PRECIOUS STONES

Their Healing Power and Planetary Influence

Magda Palmer

St. Martin's Press
New York

Library of Congress Cataloging-in-Publication Data

Palmer, Magda.
    Precious stones.

    1. Gems—Miscellanea. 2. Occultism. I. Title.
BF1442.P74P35 1988   133.3′22   87-28503
ISBN 0-312-01495-3

First published in Great Britain as a Rider Book by Century Hutchinson Ltd.

First U.S. Edition

10 9 8 7 6 5 4 3 2 1

This book is dedicated to all
those named in the list of
acknowledgements

Contents

Introduction   ix

Part One: The Planets   1
Jewels of the Zodiac   3
Solar System   10
  The Sun   10
  The Moon   12
  Mercury   13
  Venus   14
  Mars   15
  Jupiter   16
  Saturn   17
  Uranus   19
  Neptune   20
  Pluto   21

Plates   22

Part Two: Sign by Sign and Stone by Stone   25

Aries (20 March–18 April)   27
Taurus (19 April–19 May)   32
Gemini (20 May–20 June)   38
Cancer (21 June–21 July)   44
Leo (22 July–21 August)   49
Virgo (22 August–21 September)   55
Libra (22 September–22 October)   61
Scorpio (23 October–21 November)   66
Sagittarius (22 November–20 December)   73
Capricorn (21 December–19 January)   80
Aquarius (20 January–18 February)   87
Pisces (19 February–19 March)   93

CONTENTS

Part Three: Healing Stones   101
    Healing Stones   103
    Precious Health, Precious Stones   103
    Energy through Colour   108
    Care and Cleaning   109
    Esoteric Cleansing   113
    A Technique for Meditation   114

Precious Stones, Precious Health: The Healing Stones:
Alexandrite   117
Amber   117
Amethyst   119
Aquamarine   119
Aventurine   120
Azurite   121
Bloodstone   121
Blue John   122
Bowenite   123
Carnelian   123
Chalcopyrite & Bornite   123
Chrysocolla & The Eilat Stone   124
Chrysoprase   125
Citrine   125
Coral   126
Diamond   126
Dioptase   128
Emerald   129
Garnet   130
Heliodore   130
Jade & Jadeite   131
Jasper   132
Jet   132
Labradorite   133
Lapis Lazuli   133
Magnetite   134
Moonstone   135
Obsidian   135
Opal   136
Pearl   138
Peridot   139
Rhodocrosite   139

Rhodonite   139
Rock Crystal   140
Rose Quartz   141
Ruby   141
Sapphire   142
Sodalite   143
Spinel   143
Topaz   144
Tourmaline   144
Turquoise   145
Zircon   146

Glossary of Stones in Healing   148
Anniversaries   158
Envoi   165
Acknowledgements   167
Bibliography   169
List of suppliers   171

Introduction

When I was twelve, my Australian father took me to visit the famous Jenolan Caves in the Blue Mountains of New South Wales. One of the most amazing limestone caverns is known as The Cathedral, and its acoustics are so perfect that a person standing at one end has only to utter a word or sing a few notes and every soft syllable can be heard perfectly throughout the whole vast area. I remember my father, a professional singer, giving a rendering of Gounod's 'Ave Maria' to prove this point for the benefit of the rest of the party.

But it was not this aspect of the caves which won my admiration, but the great, breath-taking columns of stalagmites and stalactites, all still imperceptibly growing, though I did not understand this at the time. Their refracted colours, from orange and pink to the softest yellow and a gleaming gold, gave them the appearance of huge, luscious ice creams. They were my first introduction to the world of minerals which has entranced me ever since.

This book is about gems, which are minerals in their most refined form. It will tell you how to use as well as to appreciate them; how to discover which are the right ones for you, according to your birthsign and your physical and spiritual needs; how to enlist them as healing agents for yourself and others. My work as a consultant for Harrods store in London and for individual healers and astrologers in Britain and elsewhere has shown me how significantly the whole study of precious stones has broadened out in recent years. Gone are the days when the traditional lore concerning them was dismissed as mere superstition, when all that donors and recipients saw in them was superficial beauty, wonderful though that can be, and all that interested them was the price. Now there are even surgeons who like to have a nest of crystals placed nearby when they are carrying out operations – though few of them will yet admit the fact.

Science has stepped in to revalidate many ancient beliefs, to reinterpret the links between the planets and ourselves, and to show stones for what they are, essential mediators between outer space, ourselves and earth.

This then is the moment to look at gems with a fresh eye. The aim of this book is to help the reader to do so, adding thereby to the store of knowledge and pleasure, the spiritual enlightenment and physical well-being and health, that all of us would like to attain.

PART ONE

The Planets

Jewels of the Zodiac

It was six thousand years ago, in ancient Mesopotamia, that first the Sumerians and then the inhabitants of Ur of the Chaldees started looking at minerals and precious stones, as well as at the stars, with a view to improving their crops, protecting themselves from enemies, human or natural, foreseeing the future and generally attempting to probe the secrets of the universe – about which they knew more than our materialistic age gives them credit for. At that time the roles of priest, doctor, seer, astronomer and astrologer were merged into one. These sages knew much about the Dog-Star Sirius (Sirius A, as it is now called), and its companion star, Sirius B, despite the fact that these two bodies are right outside our solar system. (Certain primitive tribes, far removed from Mesopotamia, knew about them too, and believed that messengers from the Sirius system had descended to Earth to teach their ancestors good govern-ment and a system of counting). The Sumerians knew about the great density of Sirius B, about its fifty-year orbit round Sirius A, and because Sirius A is the brightest star in the night sky, linked both it and its accompanying star with the indigo-blue mineral, Lapis Lazuli, which they also allocated to their gods.

But this was not the end of the Sumerians' esoteric knowledge. They cut, polished and set such hard and precious substances as Rock Crystal, Amethyst and Banded Agate; they used beautiful stones to adorn their buildings and statues, and to accompany the royal and wealthy to the grave. They had also begun to grasp, though in a different way from ourselves, the general connections between Planet Earth and the rest of the solar system and the function of minerals as a link between the two.

Their method of making these connections was by colour: rose and scarlet stones to match the rusty-red tint of Mars, which mounted the horizon in April, when the Sumerian year began; green jewels for Venus, which appeared as the crops started and the people settled down to enjoy the green plenty of summer; blue for Mercury, lord of blue skies and balmy days;

violet tints for autumnal Saturn; and pale blue to reflect the melting snows on far-off mountains which occurred during Jupiter's reign. To the Sun were allocated all yellow stones, and to the Moon pearls and sea-shells fetched or traded from the Persian Gulf.

Over-simplified though these associations undoubtedly were, and misleading in many respects, they were intelligent interpretations of the facts then known (chemistry, the basis of modern matching, was unknown); and the lore of the inhabitants of ancient Mesopotamia, inherited by the Egyptians and later echoed in the Old and New Testaments, laid foundations of knowledge on which we can still build. The question to be asked in the scientific climate of today is, how can links between precious stones and the planets be shown to be genuine?

To answer this question we should reflect first of all on the fact that the ninety or so elements that constitute all matter on Earth, including minerals and the human body, are represented out there in the planets, as are Earth's minerals themselves. Thus not only is it true that no man is an island, but no planet is an island either, and our bodies reverberate to celestial vibrations through the medium of precious stones. If you stand near the wall of a room and clap your hands, the disturbance will ruffle a feather placed on a table near the wall opposite. Just so will planetary forces ruffle – or soothe – human beings. Putting the matter another way, it could be said that a precious stone will fulfil the role of an electrical substation, receiving the heat and vibrations from its owner's planetary ruler and transmitting them with increased power.

Scientific evidence suggests that all things are one, in the sense that all the chemicals and elements on Earth and on other planets are particles of our galaxy, the incredible Milky Way, which could well contain over one hundred million other solar systems besides our own, all born with the universe at the moment of the 'Big Bang', the hypothetical creative instant. Thus, throughout our lives, we have the 'melody' of our ruling planets in our bodies, and never is this planetary influence so strong as at the moment when we are born and are forcing our way into the world. Both mother and child need their appropriate stones near them at that time, to strengthen the planetary influences even further. And these influences remain.

Another argument can be drawn from the activity of nature,

even of inorganic nature. Minerals can probably boast the most spectacular and protracted pre-natal history of any substance there is. When a miner or prospector discovers a gem lying in the Earth it has not been there in that state for ever. On the contrary, it has been subjected several times, and over a period of millions of years, to a devastating alternation of expansion and shrinkage, heat and cold, brought about by the giant upheavals of the earth. There are four substances that are loosely termed mineral but belong in fact to the animal or vegetable kingdom. Two of them are Amber and Jet. They are found in the earth's crust and can be cut and polished like stone. The other two are Coral and Pearl. These come from water and water creatures. True minerals are different. Inorganic in composition, they contain exactly those elements to be found in every piece of matter in the solar system, from planets and moons, asteroids, comets and meteorites down to mere dust. Therefore, though formed on our planet, they are directly linked with their corresponding elements in celestial bodies other than Earth.

This mysterious process of creation is still going on. While we stand surveying a beautiful stretch of countryside, enjoying the shade of a forest, or getting our breath back at the top of a steep hill, minerals are constantly assembling under our feet, just as they are still being produced in the planetary masses. The correspondence between this activity on Earth and in the planets is another reason why we should try to live in harmony with them both.

The main part of this chapter will be devoted to listing and describing the stones appropriate for those born under each sign of the zodiac, but first some explanations are necessary. As will be seen, this section is divided not into signs but into half signs – first half Scorpio, second half Pisces, and so on. It is often forgotten that when the science of astrology was first devised, each sign of the zodiac filled an exact month – Capricorn filled January, Aquarius February, and so on. Down the centuries, in the course of each celestial mass's journey round the Sun, the heavenly bodies have crept into different positions, so that now each sunsign begins earlier than the first day of its original month and ends part-way through it. The dates given in this book are correct for 1988. They will continue to vary thereafter from year to year.

In the light of this, and to ensure the most accurate predictions possible, conscientious astrologers take care to consult the astronomers' annual almanack, or calendar. As the heavenly bodies move forward on their journey round the Sun, the ruler of each zodiac sign varies in the degree of influence it exerts on Earth at any given moment, hence the need for the designation of 'mutable' (that is, changeable) areas. To take Aries as an example: although its main ruler is Mars, its first half has overtones of the Sun while the second has a subsidiary ruler in Jupiter; likewise the Mercury-ruled house of Gemini has overtones of Venus in the first half with a Uranian influence in the second.

Next, it will be noted that each division of the zodiac is allotted not one classification of stones but three – its 'precious crystal', its 'talisman' and its 'bedside rock'. In rough and ready terms, these represent three orders of value, precious crystals being, as their name implies, the most precious, suitable for setting as jewellery or being carried in the pocket, preferably wrapped in silk. Next comes the talisman, a lucky charm, as the dictionaries tell us, worn to ward off evil or bring good fortune to their owner. Least costly but not least delightful is the humble bedside rock, often uncut but not for that reason less closely matched with its zodiacal sign than the other two categories – indeed, if anything, more so. The two or more choices of stone offered in almost every entry allow wearers to indulge their tastes – also to accommodate their purchases to their pockets and not be floored if some stones are hard to obtain. No one should be deprived of the chance to wear lovely gems or build up a collection of them. Using the appropriate stones in any of the ways here indicated will contribute to your general well being by putting you more closely in tune with the energies of your astrological sign and its ruling planet.

Although this book is about the beneficient powers of stones, rather than their aesthetic qualities (though these are often referred to), and is not intended as a compendium for dealers, a few definitions may be found helpful. Common or garden minerals are generally called stones (that is, anything loose and detachable from the surface of the earth), but when two or more minerals of set but distinct composition join together, the resulting formations are called rocks. Stones suitable for cutting or wearing are called gemstones, and are few in comparison with all the minerals to be found on Earth. Yet Nature is prodigal in her production of these too, and while most varieties have been known for thousands of years, new types of existing species appear from time to time, and occasionally a completely new gem is discovered, amid much rejoicing and excitement. Several are listed and described in the following pages.

The value of gemstones depends as a rule on their beauty, rarity and durability. The greater their price, the more they show Nature's magic, for she manages to make the most glittering and glorious stones out of the commonest basic materials. A Diamond is no more than crystalline common carbon. The most famous mineral of all, Rock Crystal, is simply a clear variety of Quartz, made up of two of the world's most abundant substances, silicon and oxygen. Rubies and Sapphires are a mixture of aluminium and oxygen, with traces of different metals causing their colour variations. Indeed colour in gemstones is itself a further paradox, for with one or two exceptions (notably Tourmaline and Opal) those glorious tints which add so much to pleasure and price are the result not of some natural grand design but of accidental impurities. (Amethyst, for instance, is basically Rock Crystal, its purple tint caused by an impurity in the form of iron.) To be distinguished from colour is lustre, which depends on reflection and the nature of a stone's surface. Turquoise has a waxy lustre, Diamonds and Zircons have a hard lustre, Moonstones appear silky, and so on.

The beneficial action of stones is automatic. Because their atomic structure is always the same, they will help you equally whether they are cut or uncut, mounted or unmounted, worn, carried about, or lying on a table or desk. They will do so even when the planets with which they are matched are furthest away from the earth, though the closer the better, of course.

Nor is it true that the only stones you can usefully wear are the ones astrologically matched with your planet. Nobody is under the rule of one planet alone. We are a mixture of many elements, and everything that goes on in the solar system affects everything that happens on Earth, in one way or another. So relax. Let your stones work for you, however 'passive' you or they may seem. If you want to be busy, the best thing you can do is to 'orchestrate' your collection of stones, composing them into beautiful groupings, patterns of interesting colours and shapes. That way, they will work on each other, and on you at the same time. Your stones are there to tune you into your planet, and that is all.

Finally, reference will be made in the following pages to the Mohs scale of hardness. By this form of measurement the Diamond scores highest, with a mark of ten out of ten; talc is lowest, at one out of ten. The Mohs is a purely practical test devised by a Viennese mineralogist called Friedrich Mohs, more than a century and a half ago, for the benefit of dealers and others for their own specialist purposes, and still applied, despite diversity between numbers. What concerns us here is the esoteric use to which the numbers on the Mohs scale and other numbers can be put. To explain these, we will end these introductory remarks with:

A Note on Numerology

In simple terms, the law of numerology – 'the study of the occult significance of numbers' (Webster's Dictionary) – states that all numbers are single and lie between the digits one and nine inclusive. Thus the number 10, comprising two digits, is broken down to a single number by adding together its first and second digits, one and zero, to arrive at the calculation $1 + 0 = 1$. On the same principle, 23 becomes five $(2 + 3 = 5)$, but nineteen becomes 1 by the addition of an extra step: first, add one and nine $(1 + 9 = 10)$, then add one and zero $(1 + 0 = 1)$. Final score: 1.

So far, so easy. But now we need to know the number allotted by astrological tradition to each of the heavenly bodies in our solar system. They are as follows: The Sun, 1; The Moon, 2; Jupiter, 3; Uranus, 4; Mercury, 5; Venus, 6; Neptune, 7; Saturn, 8; Mars, 9.

Pluto, on account of its very recent discovery (1930), has no traditional number, but Western astrologers, by a near unanimity, seem to be settling for the double digit 22. So that number, plus its multiples of 2, 3 and 4 – that is, 44, 66 and 88 – are treated as special cases and all are attached exclusively to this planet-come-lately.

In the following pages, listing jewels and their stars, certain numerological associations deriving from these numberings will be mentioned from time to time, in connection with the Mohs scale of hardness. It will be pointed out, for example, that Diamonds, with a hardness of 10 on the Mohs scale, are linked with the Sun $(1+0=1)$ as well as with Neptune, on which these jewels are thought to proliferate. Pink Sapphire (hardness 9) corresponds with Mars (astrological number 9); Peridot (hardness 5) goes with Mercury (astrological number 5); and so on.

In the section on anniversaries towards the end of this book (pp. 158–164) the numerical calculation is crucial. An eleventh birthday falls under the influence of the Moon $(1+1=2$, the Moon's number), a twenty-seventh under Mars $(2+7=9)$, a sixty-sixth under Jupiter $(6+6=12=3)$. So ancient astrological lore and a branch of esoteric mathematics (now adapted to the needs of the practical computer age, incidentally) combine in keeping man in harmony with the universe, the greatest boon he can enjoy.

The Solar System

'The planets in their radiant courses', as the poet felt inspired to write of them, are less romantically described in Hutchinson's invaluable 'New 20th Century Encyclopaedia' as 'non-luminous globes revolving around the Sun at various distances and in various periods'.

Five (in addition to our own Planet Earth) have been known since the earliest times. Three are newcomers. Uranus was discovered two centuries ago, Neptune in 1846, and Pluto as recently as 1930. Since then science has taken an even more spectacular hand, beginning with the Mariner II space probe of 1962 which transformed our knowledge of Venus. Soon the mysteries of Mars may be partially unveiled at least. And that is not to mention the first real Man on the Moon . . . .

Before getting down to the detailed listing of stones and signs, the reader is invited to take a journey into space, beginning, as is proper, with our own Sun and Moon, and working outwards to almost unimaginable distances. Mercury spins at 57·91 million kilometres (36 million miles) from the Sun, a mere stone's throw by astronomical standards and plainly visible. Pluto, poised on the very edge of our solar system, is no more than a speck in the scientist's telescope and over a hundred times more remote.

But near or far, all planets are equal, astrologically speaking, in terms of their actual power. These pages will explain why they differ in terms of influence.

The Sun

The Sun is our day-time star, just one among a hundred billion in the galaxy of the Milky Way, and is mostly composed of the gases hydrogen and helium, hydrogen having been converted to helium by natural nuclear reactions within the Sun's body. Scientists class the Sun as rather an ordinary medium-size star because it has shown relative stability during the past three billion years, even though it constantly wobbles, shakes, bubbles and rolls, and presents us with a vast variety of confusing surface features such as 'sunspots' (magnetic storms), 'flares' (violent outbursts) and weird atmospheric structures. Deep in its heart this blazing, spherical inferno has a natural dynamo which reverses itself every eleven years, ensuring, through its output of energy, the continuance of explosive fires which heat and light all surrounding planets, moons and matter at a range of some 5,900 million kilometres (3,687 million miles).

At more than 300,000 times the size of Earth and nearly 100 times that of every planet, satellite and solid object in our section of the Milky Way put together, the Sun has a diameter of 1,392,530 kilometres (870,331 miles). So mighty is its attraction that all the bodies in its domain dance round it like courtiers in attendance on their king. The planet we inhabit is third in distance from the Sun, preceded by Venus and Mercury and followed by Mars, Jupiter, Saturn, Uranus, Neptune and Pluto, the last mentioned being, as far as we know, the furthest away and on the very edge of the solar system. The temperature at the Sun's core has been estimated at about seventeen million degrees Centigrade and the surface heat evaluated at 5,500 degrees. Therefore the Sun has no affinity with water.

A Corona, which is a luminous envelope of ionized gases, circles the Sun and from it the 'solar wind', which is a stream of boiling atoms containing our solar system's 92 known elements, showers out at hundreds of kilometres per second. The solar wind has been employed by NASA as a relatively inexpensive form of inter-stellar travel. The Sun is sometimes called the 'solar bulb' because it makes all things visible and is our natural form of light, its white rays holding a combination of every colour of the rainbow, from red and orange through yellow and green to blue, indigo and violet. Each tint has its own frequency wave and gives a visible display only when interference breaks the merging of the spectrum.

The one zodiac sign under the sovereignty of the Sun is Leo. Though recognized by both Indian and Western astrologers, it is the Western school that conferred on it its Leonine designation, calling it 'The Lion' and allotting 'Fire' as its primary substance.

The Moon

The lunar world is aptly dubbed 'The Sea of Tranquillity', for on its erosion-free surface nothing is ever disturbed. From the cosmic rubble of ages to the footprints of the Apollo astronaut, all is still there, and will be for billions of years.

There is evidence that eruptive activity occurred in Moon's remote past, but that was before this sleeping beauty became the gentle, persuasive counterpart to bustling Earth – indeed, it was before Earth even existed. Without our lunar dancing partner we should have no gravitational energy to draw and deplete the waters of our world; nor would our dark evenings be lit by a silvery reflection of the Sun's light.

Romantic fiction turned to fact when actual pictures of the ghostly white landscape with its stark mountain ranges, deep winding canyons, flat plains of lava and vast, circular craters left by ancient bombarding meteorites, came back to us via satellite control. The Moon, over which the fabled cow once jumped, was no longer merely an inaccessible light in the sky.

To scientists the Moon is a sort of 'Space Museum' from which dust can be gathered and analysed to assist in discovering secrets of the solar system's history. Its airless surface has trapped billions of tons of solar atoms, still as fresh as at the moment when, three billion Earth-years ago, they were carried over by the solar wind. Green crystalline rock fragments, formed an estimated four million years ago, and shiny, transparent black crystals hiding in a moon-rock three and a half million years old, look fresher now in the space scientist's photograph than would a much younger stone spat from a volcano on Earth. On our planet these minerals would long since have been eroded by one thing the Moon lacks – our water, or H_2O.

Less romantically then, the Moon is a battered, lifeless globe formed separately from Earth and with one side always facing us. Earth may have captured it through gravitational pull, but that cannot be known. Still, we do at least know that it is not made of cheese and that the Man in the Moon about whom we told our children so many stories is a figment of our imagination – alas!

The Moon has many minerals similar to our own. They contain silicon, calcium, iron, titanium and magnesium, but not lead, sodium or potassium. It also reveals particles of orange soil which are really minute glass beads formed through a former burst of intense heat. It has plentiful rocks, mostly composed of a sort of feldspar. Its diameter measures 3,476 kilometres, or 2,160 miles, a mere quarter of that of Earth.

Both Indian and Western astrologers agree that Cancerians are Moon-ruled. Water is their element, because the Moon controls the tides and all 'the waters under the Earth', as the Bible puts it, including the preponderance of water in our own bodies, and their accepted emblem is the Crab.

Mercury

Covered by a colourless coating of pummelled rock-dust, planet Mercury's perilous position as the Sun's closest neighbour shows in its bleached, pock-marked face and rough, cratered body. Corresponding with the pitch-black Mercurian sky, satanic shadows mark the rise of intensely lit white hills while shimmering plains spread below cliff paths curling and zig-zagging a thousand metres above. This pale, confused landscape is shaped by volcanic action and major shrinkage which occurred long ago in Mercury's distant past while dark glassy lava regions display pitted rock where the planet's lighter material has been baked by the Sun's splitting rays.

This is the eastern, Sun-scorched side of the planet, with a day temperature of 400 degrees Centigrade. In direct contrast, and as if touched by an angel, is the western side, this time exposed to Venus, in which evening covers the brutal countryside with a saintly shroud of dark grey and the temperature drops dramatically to minus 183 degrees Centigrade. The setting Sun's tenacious fingers throw skyward streamers of blue, gold and green which fly into distant space till they eventually fuse in aerial flight. Our Earth and Moon are seen as twin blue stars and the light of bright planet Venus shines with cut-crystal clarity, casting hypnotic shadows over the lulled land. The solar wind replenishes Mercury's surface with helium.

The waterless, metallic mineral world has an ultra-slow axis spin which lengthens each day and night to the equivalent of nearly fifty-nine complete rotations of Earth, yet its 87·969 Earth day year is the shortest in the solar system. Sprinting alone through space on an eccentric orbit, this planet has no companion moon. The smallest globe in our heaven (at 4,878 km or 3,049 miles in diameter), except probably for Pluto, Mercury is fittingly named after the swift messenger of the gods, son of almighty Zeus and of Maia, the goddess of Night.

By Indian astrological lore, Gemini comes under the domain of Mercury's light side and Virgo under its dark. Astrologers of the Western school also place these two signs in Mercury's charge. Virgo's emblem is a woman with the element earth. Gemini's is the twins, Artemis and Apollo, children of Zeus, who inhabit air.

Venus

As the only planet named after a female in our male-orientated solar system, Venus shows its individuality by making its days last longer than its years. It obtains this result by rotating at a snail's pace, making each individual day equivalent to about 226 Earth days. Yet the comparatively giddy speed at which it circles the Sun would cut Earth's year to 224·7 days. Its slow rotation has another unusual effect. Venus is the only world to have an even temperature day and night.

This steamy, torrid namesake of the Roman goddess of Love has a surface heat of about 425 degrees Centigrade, hot enough to melt lead. Its drab, grey terrain has a strong orange cast and is constantly threatened by sulphuric rain from a highly charged electrical sky whence lightning and thunder precede gales of typhoon-like violence which bully and catapult cart-sized boulders over a punch-drunk surface. Yet suddenly this volatile mistress of heaven can undergo a change of attitude and, although the globe remains flaming hot, light winds caress the broken rocks and stones of lava, salt and sulphur.

Estimated to measure 12,104 kilometres (or 7,565 miles) across and with an atmospheric density about 100 times that of Earth, planet Venus gathers and traps heat and light, re-radiating precious little to its tiny neighbour Mercury.

Mexican mythologists used to say of their major god: 'After his death Quetzalcoatl's heart rose to become silver Venus.' From Earth, this perfectly shaped second world from the Sun appears heavily veiled by a curtain of cloud and water, its smooth, whitish orb pocked with craters, valleys and volcanoes, the whole resembling an austere, waterless sea-bed.

Both Indian and Western astrologers consider Taurus and Libra to be ruled by Venus. Western sages allot the Bull of Minos as the Taurean emblem and Earth as its simple body, or element, while Libra's emblem is the Scales of Justice and its element is air.

Mars

Though named after the god of war, Mars is in fact a curiously peaceful planet which boasts a fragile atmosphere and soft, scattered clouds in a salmon-pink sky. Blissful winds whose gentleness belies their speed (24 kilometres or 15 miles per hour) brush over the mid-green terrain with its cracked craters peppered with meteorite scars. They are hurrying to reach the other side of the planet where the undulating landscape comprises crushed strawberry-coloured sand dunes with bracken-tinted shadows. In contrast to its arthritic-looking green side, here the setting Sun will illuminate and light the rock masses and bronze the ribbons of dry river-beds which coil their way through pinky-brown deserts for hundreds of kilometres, fading at last into tributary arms which reach into snow-capped mountains.

Mars is always much colder than Earth, with an afternoon temperature at the Equator no higher than 26 degrees Centigrade. The Martian evening is truly dark, for the planet's two moons, Phobos and Deimos, are fashioned from sombre, irregular lumps of matter. However, at 7.30 a.m. local time a theatrically lit early morning will find the peak of a colossal, extinct volcano called Olympus Mons (25 kilometres or 15 miles high) looking down on an orchestral space-dance in which the performers are frolicking patches of blue and green vapour disappearing into a pink heaven from the valleys and crater basins. The valleys' fluted edges recall wind and rain erosion on Earth but there is no water here. Maybe there once was because the clay-like soil is coloured by rusted iron and the rocks are similar to the sulphur and water compounds and the lava found on Earth. Sadly, however, this fourth globe from the Sun and the planet most favoured by science fiction writers past and present gives no indication of ever having supported life as we know it on Earth.

Yet Mars was once Earth-like and both planets have many similarities. Although one Martian year is the equivalent of twenty-three months on Earth, both take approximately 24 hours to rotate on their axes, each enjoys four seasons and has ice-caps which aren't quite centred on their North and South poles. Mars has a rotational 30-degree tilt similar to that of Earth, although its diameter is smaller at 6,794 kilometres (4,246 miles), against Earth's 12,756 kilometres (7,972 miles) and our Moon's 3,476 kilometres (2,172 miles).

Pink is the colour of impartial love and blue Earth's immediate neighbour on the outer side of the Sun shines for us with softer brilliance than Venus does on her Sun-side.

Indian astrologers say Mars shows its pink side for Aries and its green side for Scorpio. Western astrologers place Mars as the Arian ruling planet, designate the golden-fleeced ram (Mars spelt backwards without the 's') as the sign's emblem and give 'fire' as its substance. For them Scorpio comes under the domain of Pluto with an added sub-influence of Mars.

Jupiter

Positioned in the dynamic middle path of the solar system, belching huge aerial waves, Jupiter well deserves its occasional nickname of 'Enraged Bull of the Universe'. Its gyrating mass abounds in swirling tints of yellow, black and brown, relieved by smaller patches of mid-blue and pink. A vehement storm in the guise of a great red spot has menaced its anguished face for the past three hundred years. Named after the Roman equivalent of the great god Zeus, lord of the thunderbolts and giver of victory, this titanic ball with the density of very weak gravy shows unremitting fury at its dismissal to outer space.

In Jupiter's immediate sky, rapid, whining wind-changes tear wretched clouds to pathetic excuses, while from the depths of its gaseous atmosphere feathery plumes of some vivid, unknown substance throw intense and immeasurable ultra-violet light, promising death to any Earthman insolent enough to venture there.

Above the mêlée and like a flock of frightened angels, five large alabaster-coloured moons float in semi-stillness. These frozen combinations of ammonia, carbon dioxide and nitrogen glitter and gleam as spidery webs of crackling orange and blue electrical currents flick icy spangles from their frosty mantles. Also witnessing their master's wrath are about thirteen unattached moons.

Io is Jupiter's principal satellite and queen. It glows bright red and yellow due to the presence of iron and sulphur elements formed from the first active volcanoes found outside Earth. Myriad shimmering golden haloes crown its surface and can be seen through the telescope reflected intermittently in white snow patches patterning its otherwise charred, jet-black terrain.

Jupiter is the largest planet in the solar system. At the enormous measurement of 142,800 kilometres (89,500 miles) it has a diameter more than eleven times that of Earth and is an astonishing 3,018 times greater in mass. Its rotational spin takes just under ten hours, against Earth's 24, though it takes nearly twelve years to make its journey round the Sun. Seen from our planet it glows with a steady, yellow-based, blue-green light – a deceptive appearance of calm. It is hideously cold.

Both Indian and Western astrologers place Sagittarians and Pisceans in the Jovian domain, but Western sages find only Sagittarians to be completely ruled by Jupiter. They give the Archer cum Centaur as its emblem and 'Fire' as its essence. Pisceans, though co-ruled by Jupiter, are more subject to Neptune.

Saturn

A great, golden brown balloon surrounded by speeding circular bands of luminous light looking like rainbows – such is the appearance of Saturn, 'the Charmer of the Universe'. No other world can compare with this illustrious masterpiece (diameter 120,000 kilometres or 75,000 miles), named after the second oldest deity of the Roman Empire, who was also the god of fertility.

Nine or so hoops or bands festoon this planet. They are made up of thousands of miniature moons fashioned from cosmic dust which reflect the Sun's light through their coating of frozen gases. None of these moons is more than a hundred kilometres (sixty-two and a half miles) across; some are as little as ten kilometres (six and a quarter miles). They speed in their own orbits round planet Saturn which itself takes approximately 10,759·26 Earth days, or 29·46 Earth years, to circle the Sun. Because of this slow, deliberate trudge, or perhaps because it was named after an aged god, Saturn has suffered from mistaken classifications and been wrongly identified with heavy corresponding Earth minerals. In fact this gossamer globe has the lightest bodyweight of all planets in our area of the Milky Way and very pretty shadows of bright indigo and deep violet mark its whitish and yellow-brown surface with fuzzy-edged patches.

A most unusual feature of Saturn's sky is an extra-long, ribbon-like cloud which floats below at least twenty extravagantly fashioned water-ice moons of much larger proportions than those fairy domains which comprise its reflective rings.

Being so far from the Sun, Saturn is dimly lit, although it is easy to see a small, revolving red spot which stalks its face and is thought to be a threatening storm. Its weather conditions seem stable, however, doubtless because this sixth world in our planetary system emits uninterruptedly and at a constant rate three times the amount of heat it receives from the Sun. After this incredible world the solar wind finishes its journey, sprinkling its ebbing strength from the Sun on the nine gyrating haloes whose billions of rainbows effectively crown Saturn with more jewels than any king could acquire.

Indian astrologers give Aquarians and Capricorns a Saturnian ruling, but their Western counterparts allow only the latter to come under Saturn alone, placing Aquarians, to whom they nonetheless concede a Saturnian sub-influence, under the sign of Uranus. So Aquarians reading this book must look under Uranus for their minerals. For Capricorns, the Western school designates the Sea-Goat as their emblem and Earth as their substance.

Uranus

The glacial temperature on Uranus is hardly friendly at minus 180 degrees Centigrade but the icy sunlight, roughly 1,000 times brighter than that of the full moon on Earth, invites strange reveries. All shades of green, from lettuce through Sherwood to olive, suffuse the planet's genteel hollows, making them appear deeper, while airborne icicles, similarly coloured, suggest fairy-tale forests.

This green giant, its girth measuring 51,800 kilometres (32,375 miles) contains traces of the odourless, low temperature, lighter-than-air gas Methane, a major constituent of natural gas and petroleum, and on Earth often found near water. Many scientists have consequently been tempted to deduce the presence of water on Uranus, and also that the planet produces oxygen, carbon, nitrogen, silicon and iron. These in turn produce between them hydrogen, helium, methane and ammonia.

No internal heat emanates from this extraordinary globe, which, like a tubby man who can't rise after a fall, rolls sideways during the 85 Earth years, or approximately 31,053 days, that it takes to circle the Sun. Believe it or not, the warmest place on this planet is probably either its North or its South Pole, rather than its Equator.

Uranus's sky has two largish moons crowned by shimmering, ice-frosted haloes. Named after the fairy king and queen in Shakespeare's A Midsummer Night's Dream, they faithfully act out their parts, the jealous and conceited Oberon not wanting the exquisite Titania to outshine him, and the proud queen not giving way, so that they both hurl effervescent bubbles of light far beyond themselves, propelling toxic vivacity towards the Sun.

Three smaller satellites are in attendance on Titania and Oberon. There is Umbriel, who betrays his presence by no more than a shy sparkle, Miranda in her dark cloak, and Ariel, who tries to win the admiration of the royal couple by throwing out shiny bubbles. Above them the watchful black rings of Uranus, seventh world from the Sun, arc narrow and steady, a reminder that this planet was named after the father of the antique gods, who with his wife Ge (Earth) brought forth the Titans, the Cyclops, the Furies and other terrifying creatures of mythology. Uranus was discovered by Herschel, court astronomer to King

George III, who wrote that he was renaming the planet George, since 'it first shone officially in his auspicious reign. God save the King'. The result was laughter, followed by a protracted stalemate. Was this new planet to be called by the name of its discoverer, the king, or the most ancient of the gods? It took sixty years to decide.

Indian astrologers do not recognize Uranus, but Western seers place Aquarius under its domain. They allocate air as the Aquarian substance and the Water Bearer as its symbol.

Neptune

This planet, discovered in 1846, appears to be covered by an ocean of swelling waves capped by oodles of perfectly formed diamonds which shimmer in the light of the distant Sun. This fairy-tale description may sound far-fetched, but in fact the latest density measurements of Neptune's surface prove that it cannot be made of gases like most of the outer planets but must consist of very hot water surrounding a rocky core which itself is about six times the size of our Earth.

Neptune's diamonds would be composed of the same chemicals and elements as those on Earth, and most likely the planet is rich in them. The secret of their probable existence lies in the frozen methane gas which, with a number of other constituents still unidentified, forms the white bands which encircle Neptune's face and the clouds which pattern its sky. When methane atoms are broken down, they become carbon. This in its turn, when compressed under great heat and pressure, becomes the pure substance of diamonds. And so the presence of diamonds on Neptune may reasonably be deduced.

This planet, with a diameter of 50,540 kilometres (31,400 miles), is a fast mover, with a spin producing a day and night of, respectively, sixteen and eighteen hours. However, it takes it 164·80 Earth years to complete its trip around the Sun. The rapidity of this spin causes pressure to build up, first, on the planet's slightly flattened top and base and, secondly, on its two sides. So the idea of this planet as a glittering, pale blue balloon, poised in space and encircled by white hoops, is scientifically sound as well as artistically satisfying.

Satisfying too, to science fiction buffs at least, is the thought that if unspeakable catastrophe struck planet Earth, the best place to move to would be Triton, Neptune's largest moon, for this satellite has an earth-like atmosphere possibly capable of supporting human life. Unfortunately Triton rotates in an alarmingly precarious fashion, lurching backwards and off-centre, with the consequence that this suicidal mass is likely to disintegrate (though perhaps not for ten, or even a hundred, million years) as it draws too near to its own planet, Neptune. In the meantime man could just possibly make some use of the earth-like iron and silicon minerals on Triton's rocky terrain, its cratered landscape reminding him of Earth's moon.

Neptune is the eighth world in distance from the Sun, and is named after the old Roman god of the Sea, whose Greek counterpart was Poseidon. Triton, son of Neptune and of Amphitrite, pleasing goddess of the sea, is represented in legend as a fish with a human head. In the world of planets, with a diameter of 35,000 kilometres (21,875 miles), or just less than three-quarters that of Neptune, Triton is immense in comparison with our Moon, which is only about a quarter the size of Earth.

Neptune is disregarded by Indian astrologers, but Pisceans are ruled by it according to the Western tradition, with a sub-influence of Jupiter. Pisceans' badge of office is two fishes joined head to tail and their primary element is water.

Pluto

On the rim of the solar system, 5,900 million kilometres (or 3,666 million miles) from the Sun, planet Pluto rotates erratically. This is the most secretive world in our area of the Milky Way. Nobody knows its chemical make-up. Nobody knows its exact size – though by calculations based on comparisons with our Moon, astronomers have estimated Pluto's diameter to be 3,000 kilometres, or 1,875 miles, maximum. At only three hundred times the strength of full moon on Earth, the far-away, midday Sun twinkles like a dazzling pin-prick in the Plutonian sky, a twilight zone on a glazed, flat, frozen surface. Hazy-purple, slate and rich red in colouring, it is rightly named after the god of the Infernal Regions, brother of Jupiter and Neptune. Charon, who ferried the souls of the dead across the Styx to Hades, lends

1. Amethyst   2. Rose Quartz   3. Rock Crystal
4. Fluorite   5. Rock Crystal

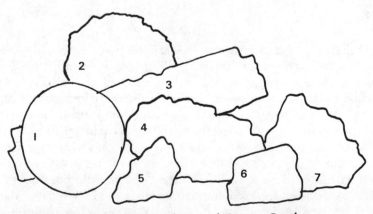

1. Geode with Amethyst   2. Calcite and Quartz Geode
3. Gypsum   4. Quartz on Hematite   5. Eilat Stone (Malachite)
6. Rhodocrosite   7. Chalcopyrite

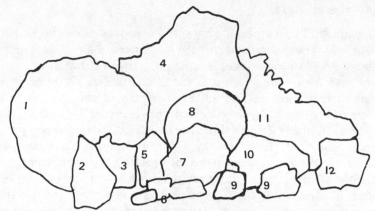

1. Sardonyx (Agate)   2. Lapis Lazuli   3. Iron Pyrites   4. Citrine
5. Moonstone   6. Tiger's Eye   7. Geode   8. Jade   9. Turquoise
10. Azurite   11. Amber   12. Smoky Quartz

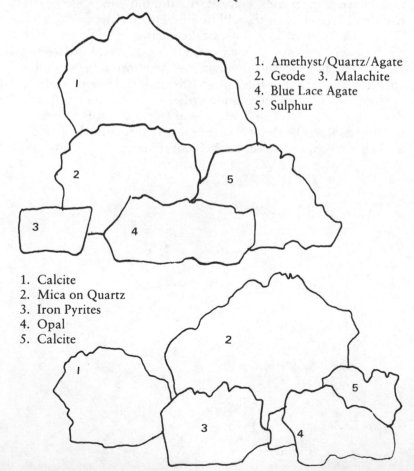

1. Amethyst/Quartz/Agate
2. Geode   3. Malachite
4. Blue Lace Agate
5. Sulphur

1. Calcite
2. Mica on Quartz
3. Iron Pyrites
4. Opal
5. Calcite

his name to Pluto's moon. This satellite moves neither to North, South, East nor West in relation to its planet but hangs stationary above it in luminous complacency, a giant in comparison with our own Moon, of which it is six times the size. Together this pair of frosty entities, which at the birth of the solar system were molten fireballs, slowly circumnavigate the Sun, taking the equivalent of 247·7 Earth years (or over 90,000 days) to complete each course. On their six-day rotational period Pluto and its moon have a hair-raising habit of crossing the orbital path of Neptune, their nearest planetary neighbour, in a sort of celestial bout of Russian Roulette, spurred on, say scientists, by the hypnotic attraction that Neptune has for Pluto's moon. Pluto and planet Earth, again according to astronomers, are the only two worlds with a double planetary system, but there the likeness between them ends, since Earth and our Moon are nearly five times further apart than Pluto and his Ferryman.

Though Western astrologers take account of Pluto, Indian practitioners dismiss it as a vulgar interloper (it was discovered as recently as 1930 and then, in the first instance, by mathematical calculation rather than direct observation). In the Western scheme this ninth and furthest planet from the Sun is designated as the ruler of Scorpio with Mars as a sub-influence. Its subjects have the Desert Scorpion – or, anciently, the Eagle – as their emblem and water as their substance.

PART TWO

Sign by Sign and Stone by Stone

First Half Aries (20 March–3 April): Precious Crystal

Pink Diamond

A 'fancy' is the term used in the diamond trade for fine quality gems exhibiting beautiful and unusual tints. One of the rarest in this class is the Pink Diamond, of which the top quality occurs in Western Australia. It is also the precious crystal which corresponds with the first half of Aries ruled by the planet Mars with the Sun as a mutable body. To deal with the mutable mass first, it should be said that a Diamond is formed of one element only and is unique in that this one element (carbon) is self-bonding when exposed to elevated temperatures and extreme pressure, after which it becomes a crystal of carbon, better known as a Diamond. The Diamond, like the Sun, has no affinity with water. It can withstand very high temperatures and, in correspondence to the Sun's light, has the highest degree of brilliance possible in a transparent material.

Nobody knows what colours some Diamonds pink, but as the first set Aries have the Sun as their mutable body and Mars as their true celestial sovereign they must have a Pink Diamond as their precious crystal. Moreover, in view of the fact that Mars has no water and that popular astrology considers the Aries individual to be ruled by the red (in reality pink) side of Mars, the Pink Diamond corresponds with this gentle planet of the rusty-pink terrain and the softly coloured pink sky down to the last detail.

A second precious crystal for first half Arians is the Pink Sapphire. Strong enough to deal with the Sun as a mutable planet at a hardness of 9 (the number allotted to Mars by numerologists) and thought to be coloured by a sniff of iron and chromium, this stone has a metallic element dominant in its composition and is one of the most intensely luminous crystals in existence.

Second Half Aries (4 April–18 April): Precious Crystal

Alexandrite

This scarce variety of the chrysoberyl family has a curious absorption of light in the critical yellow-green part of the spectrum which gives it marked hues of dark, mossy-green in daylight and soft, columbine or raspberry-red under electricity. Sometimes Alexandrite occurs in paler shades, but still exhibits the pink to green colour-change. Coloured by the metallic element chromium, it actually comprises the rare metal berylium, and also aluminium, the former giving it a correspondence with planet Jupiter, which scientists believe has rare metals swirling around in its mass. The Beryl is the only commercial source of berylium, and this, being one of the lightest metallic elements, is a bodyweight match for both Jupiter and Mars.

Because of its colour-change, the Alexandrite is often thought of as an Emerald by day and an Amethyst by night and for this peculiarity is treasured by connoisseurs. It was also much valued by a scoundrelly old womanizer of days gone by, who used it to trick innocent girls. He told them that if the Emerald they saw by day turned into an Amethyst by night it would prove his undying love for them.

Discovered on the birthday of Tsar Alexander II, and sporting the Russian national colours, the Alexandrite is the first gem of Russia. It came to light first on the banks of the Takovaya River in the Urals, but since then has been found in Brazil, Madagascar, Zimbabwe and Sri Lanka.

The tranquil gem Rhodonite is another precious crystal for Arians born in the last half. Whether transparent or translucent, this little known and rare crystal reflects the Martian rusty-pink terrain and its pink to soft rose-red sky. In sympathy with Jupiter, Rhodonite has a greenish tone when containing impurities, but its basic composition is variable in that its manganese elements can be replaced by calcium or iron. This gemstone has a medium hardness of 5·5–6·5 out of 10, but is still very wearable and quite at home with frosty Mars and with Jupiter's distance from the Sun.

Semi-precious, opaque Rhodonite with its splendid spectrum of baby-pink, crushed strawberry and raspberry tints, often seamed by a black alteration product, was favoured by Carl Fabergé, whose aristocratic clientèle commissioned petite vases of Rhodonite berries, boxes and farmyard animals. In view of this one would assume that the best quality came from Russia, but in fact top quality Rhodonite occurs in the vicinity of the hot, dusty Australian town called Broken Hill.

First Half Aries (20 March–3 April): Talisman

Sunstone

A reddish irridescence, brought about by minute inclusion of hematite, lepidocrite and like materials on a yellow or brownish-yellow background, is a characteristic of this gem. Lepidocrite is a mineral made of translucent red to orange-red crystals found in veins of iron, and hematite is a valuable iron ore. Both correspond with the Martian globe.

The Sunstone imitates the Sun by its red and gold spangled brilliance which glitters and gleams sensationally in jewellery. It is usually cut with a rounded surface or half-round.

When flecked with red, the Sunstone is called Jasper, another Arian birthstone.

An alternative talisman for these Arians is the dark-green gemstone with red flecks known as Heliotrope, a name derived from the Greek word meaning 'sun turning'. It is otherwise known as a Bloodstone. This legendary gemstone, which, it was once believed, would change the yellow of the Sun to crimson if immersed in water, has always brought its wearer good fortune. It lives with the chalcedony family which usually forms at low temperatures, making it an Earth mineral parallel to Mars in colour, composition and formation. The Red Indians, Arabs and Babylonians wore amulets of carved Bloodstone.

When Bloodstone lacks its red flecks it is called Plasma (another gemstone for the Arians in this set). The dark-green is coloured by a material known as Green Earth – which is not what its name implies but rather a mineral derived from chemicals in molten lava which are rich in both iron and manganese.

Second Half Aries (4 April–18 April): Talisman

Bowenite

The ancient Persians called it 'Sang-I-Yashim', the New Zealand Maories 'Tangiwaiit', and we know it as Bowenite, the talisman for Arians in the second half.

Previously the stones allotted as talismans to Arians have been of bright and harsh colours, perhaps through ignorance of the fact that their celestial sovereign's mass is muted, rather than brutal-red, and that the ancient side of Mars is green.

Bowenite with its soft, mystic green translucence belongs to the serpentine family of minerals, yet it is more than twice as hard as the other members of its clan at a count of 5·5. It contains the Martian metal (iron) amongst other metallic elements which correspond to that planet. Wonderful specimens occur in America, Afghanistan, China, Kashmir and New Zealand, the last mentioned country producing green Bowenite with a touch of blue which noticeably deepens that normally pale stone. For the pocket of the average person, splendid Bowenite beads, assorted jewellery and carvings are available. The carvings are generally fashioned in China and then sold as 'Chinese Jade'. Apart from this the occasional Bowenite talisman from the Punjab may be found in genuine antique shops.

Carl Fabergé commemorated the birth of Tsarevitch Nicholas, heir to the Russian throne, by designing a presentation clock of Bowenite embellished with opalescent-pink and translucent-white enamelling, rose (cut) Diamonds, silver-gilt figures and platinum doves.

Another talisman for second set Arians is a transparent tawny-red or translucent yellow-rust member of the chalcedony group known as Carnelian or Sard. Around the middle of the sixth century the Greeks and Phoenicians started using cutting wheels and drills to embellish gemstones. Carnelian was the favourite material because of its fine, granular formula, its availability and its variegated shadings, which were carefully utilized. The artist used the drill as a brush and the stone as both paint and canvas. Paler zones were meticulously worked for intricate hairstyles and the upper folds of garments, the darker tints for the face and body. A popular subject was the Egyptian scarab, worn as a ring and used as a seal. The carved ring-side of the beetle was set lengthways on a swivel, thus enabling it to be flipped over to reveal the underside engraved with personal insignia.

Carl Fabergé also enjoyed working Carnelian. Particularly magnificent is his 'Pumpkin Box', decorated with yellow-gold, white enamel and rose (cut) Diamonds.

First Half Aries (20 March–3 April): Bedside Rock

Cinnabar
For the double-sided, Martian world ruling Aries, a triple combination of bedside rocks feature scarlet Cinnabar with Dolomite and Quartz. The Neolithic artist powdered Cinnabar to colour his gory pictures of animals and the chase and its modern name derives from the Persian word for dragon's blood. In about 100 BC the Romans ordered 4,500 tons of Cinnabar from Spain, where among other places, it is still being worked today. Now it is being put to many beneficial uses. It contains up to 86 per cent Mercury and is the most important mineral bearing that metal.

The gentle Martian world with its light atmosphere is in harmony with this bedside rock's vermillion crystals and their fine, transparent edges, all the more so as Cinnabar is often found in veins near cooling volcanic disturbances, corresponding with the extinct volcanoes on Mars. In laboratory tests red Cinnabar gives off greenish fumes, their colour matching the ancient face of Mars.

Like Cinnabar, Dolomite is a soft material, transparent to translucent in appearance, and is usually tinted pearly-white or pearl-yellow – hence its other name, Pearl Spar. Its crystals are reasonably common and hard to distinguish from those of calcite. It was named after the man who first recognized the distinction, Deodat Dolomieu, in 1791. As a source of carbon dioxide it is a correct match for the Sun.

Quartz, which completes the trio of bedside rocks for first half Arians, actually corresponds with planet Saturn, but Earth's most abundant mineral is acceptable visually to complete the dramatic display of scarlet in its triple textures, providing a sparkling finish in contrast with the matt of Cinnabar and the pearl-lustred surface of Dolomite.

Second Half Aries (4 April–18 April): Bedside Rock

Youngite
Imagine a craggy mass of solid mushroom-pink shimmering with stardust, and you have Youngite, the second set Arian bedside rock. It is actually red Jasper with a re-crystallized

surface, a tough opaque material that featured strongly in the jewellery of New Kingdom Egypt (1500–900 BC). The vogue in that era was for earplugs and earrings, broad collars, double-string girdle belts, armbands, bracelets and pendants, in a colour co-ordinated mixture of seeds, glass, metal beads and various stones, the link between them being reddish Jasper which was often cut in the form of a barrel-shaped bauble. It corresponds to the soil of the planet ruling Aries which is now known to be pink in all shades.

Nature changed the appearance of this long-loved member of the chalcedony family by giving it a coating of transparent and minute rock crystals and set the 'new model' Jasper in a place where man would discover it. He found it in America and named it Youngite. It sits well to Jupiter, the mutable planet for Aries in the second half, and to the outer planets too with their cooler position in space.

As a glorious second bedside rock, fortunate Arians have the ornamental Ruby Zoisite. Looking like a bright-green cherry cake with dark chocolate bits, this gem cuts to superb dishes, ashtrays, eggs and even solitaire spheres. The cherries are actually big, blobby, opaque crystals of Ruby which are held fast in a black mineral running through the Zoisite, with its bright yellow to grass-green tints. The black mineral holding the Rubies is iron-rich. Tanzania yields this wonderfully attractive stone.

First Half Taurus (19 April–2 May): Precious Crystal

Emerald
Emeralds have a fascinating, well-charted history, going back to the earliest times. They were first found in Ethiopia and legend has it that Sargon I, Emperor of that country, always wore one. They were a prime source of wealth in ancient Egypt, and also Greece. Hieroglyphics have survived showing Greek miners at work in a mine near the Red Sea in the time of Alexander the Great – their tools were rediscovered in the early nineteenth century – and in Roman times, a famous Emerald was inscribed with Cleopatra's face.

In Latin America Peruvian temples were grass-green with Emeralds while in Mexico they were plundered in vast quantities by the Conquistadors for use, among other things, in their own churches. Today the most notable Emeralds are found in Colombia, Egypt, the Salzburg Alps, Siberia, Zambia and Zimbabwe.

The Emerald crystal always contains at least two metallic chemicals, aluminium and berylium, but its glowing and seductive tints, which run through dark, rich to paler shades of green, are probably due to the presence of small amounts of chromium. Red Emeralds have occurred in nature, but few of gem quality have ever reached the market. Large Emeralds are rare, which accounts for their high price, and so are clear specimens. Most are cloudy from imperfections and the inclusion of extraneous minerals, and the trade calls them 'mossy'. Under the microscope even absolutely clear Emeralds show a characteristic trait of uneven colour distribution, often in layers.

Although Emerald is of low bodyweight, and on this count ill-matched for the ponderous Venus, its metallic elements make amends and Taureans can own or wear one of these stones with confidence.

They can feel equally at home with the Oriental Emerald, which is actually a green Sapphire, and also contains aluminium. It is harder than the Emerald and slightly heavier, but lacks the other stone's intensity of colour. One good reason for its correspondence to Venus is that its toughness would make it impervious to acid rain.

Second Half Taurus (3 May–19 May): Precious Crystal

Andalusite
Just as a caterpillar turns into a butterfly, so Andalusite has undergone a magical-seeming change – in the case of the transparent variety, from opaque, black rock to colourful, pelucid crystal.

In the dark, amorphous interior of the Earth, waves of heat once caused areas of solidified rock to evaporate and steam their way through splits in the crust. In the process, the liquid gases mixed and transferred parts of themselves to places where they either came to rest or received more pressure as they settled to cool. Some remained as they were but most continued to somersault, melt, mix, swim and restyle themselves until they reached an area near the surface of the Earth, where they took the form they have now. A great variety of stones was the result, but Andalusite's character is determined by aluminium, which accounts for its correspondence with Venus, giving it reflective powers to match those of the brightest star in the sky. Like Venus too, it can withstand great pressures of light and heat, and is a remarkable conductor of electricity.

The Andalusite crystal presents itself in tints of yellow, green, grey, pink, flesh-red, red, purplish-red and brown, each variety displaying mineral magic in its ability to vary its shade when viewed from a different angle. A particularly lovely change is that from green to purplish-red; another is that from blue-purple to pale yellow. Both coloured and transparent crystals match Venus and Saturn, mutable planet for second half Taureans, in tone as well as hardness. Their hardness count is uneven, with a maximum rating of 7·5 and, like the Emerald, they are resistant to acid. Some gem dealers heat the Andalusite crystal for sale in the retail market as this process can turn it a bright rich blue – a colour also very appropriate for correspondence with Venus and Saturn.

Some Taureans in this area of the zodiac may prefer Andalusite's sister gem, Chiastolite, which has the same composition but with added flecks of carbon that give the impression of a four-petalled flower, or cross. In northern Spain Chiastolite crystals are accordingly called 'Stones of the Cross' and have been sold to pilgrims since medieval times. In fact Andalusite derives its name from the Spanish province of Andalusia. Today, however, top quality gems come from Brazil.

These Taureans have yet another precious crystal – Sphalerite. The richest colour of gem quality produced by this stone is a glorious brownish-gold with a play of intense yellow light, but Sphalerite can come in so many hues that not even experts always recognize it straight away. It usually contains iron along with a number of rarer elements, while non-precious sphalerite is a major ore of zinc. Top gem quality crystals generally come from Spain.

First Half Taurus (19 April–2 May): Talisman

Azurite and Malachite

These stones are the twin talismans for first half Taureans. They have similar compositions and the same hardness measure (3·5–4). Both, too, yield well over 50 per cent copper which, thanks to its content of sulphur and iron, establishes their correspondence with both Venus (ruling Taurean celestial body) and Mercury (first half mutable globe).

The intense, transparent to translucent azure-blue Azurite is the rarer stone of the two. It tends to occur either in rosettes formed of tiny powdered crystals, or in sparkling masses on minerals of other varieties.

During the 15th and 16th centuries European artists used ground Azurite extensively, but it was then discovered that, when the paint dried, the brilliant blue Azurite colour changed to various shades of stunning green Malachite.

The more prolific Malachite is easily recognized by its swirling zones of light and dark colours, dramatic patterns resembling pale-green cream in an exotic emerald nectar. Sometimes called 'Satin Ore', Malachite is the subject of many ancient, magic tales. Once upon a time, individuals in possession of this mineral were said to be able to understand the conversation of animals, and many a Russian Princess spent days of delight playing with Malachite trinket boxes filled with matching foibles, which were supposed to confer the power of invisibility upon their owner.

Don't buy ashtrays made of either of these minerals – cigarette and cigar stubs mark them. But they are popular for other ornaments. Supplies of both stones come mainly from the Congo, which yielded over 2,000 tons in 1966, but large quantities are now found in Australia, America, Britain, France and Siberia.

Second Half Taurus (3 May–19 May): Talisman

Jadeite

This stone can only be formed under high pressure – which makes it a worthy partner for planet Venus where the heavier than Earth atmosphere could crush anything. It is exceptionally resilient, with fibrous, interlocking crystals in its structure which give a toughness greater than that of steel.

Wonderful shades of Jadeite include black, brown, pink, red, orange-brown and white, through to many shades of green. The lavender shade of Jadeite has been allocated to second half Taureans because planet Saturn of the purple and blue shadows is their mutable globe.

Jadeite is the symbol of purity, steadfastness and all things enduring. When struck it gives a musical note, which is doubtless the source of ancient belief that it was a 'charm of harmonious omen'. One terrifying lady who fancied this gem was Tz'e Hsi, the tyrannical last Empress Dowager of China, who died in 1908. In her long life she is thought to have collected over 3,000 carved Jadeite containers, all choc-à-bloc with trinkets of the same stone.

A Pyritized Ammonite is an extra talisman and one sometimes so smooth that it can be carried in the pocket, placed in a locket or cut in half and set as cufflinks. This gem can be said to be history in silvered stone, for it is formed from a creature extinct for 60 million years – the early forerunner of the octopus family. Probably a vegetarian, it inflated its body with air, which enabled it to shoot through water like a modern submarine. Fine examples of Pyritized Ammonite come from Yorkshire in England, and from France. Its link with Venus is the iron ore, pyrite, which is used to produce sulphur dioxide for sulphuric acid.

First Half Taurus (19 April–2 May): Bedside Rock

Marcasite Dollar

For good reason is the Marcasite Dollar the bedside rock of first set Taureans, for it is formed in an environment of acid solutions, corresponding with Venus, the planet of sulphuric rain. It is a flat circular stone, formed of radiating and glittering crystals which vary gently in hue from silver-yellow to yellow-bronze. It is an ore of platinum, another Venusian link inasmuch as that tough, almost indestructible metal could even resist the testing conditions on that globe. But though platinum is used by jewellers, very little jewellery offered as Marcasite is the genuine article – modern trade prefers steel. 'White', to give it its geological description, the surface of this gem must, if sold as an adornment, be covered with some non-tarnishable substance or else the blaze of light which issues from its heart will become dim.

Cubes of silver-tinted Pyrite, otherwise known as Fool's Gold, is a second bedside rock for these Taureans. Pyrite's composition is identical to that of Marcasite, but this stone is formed at a higher temperature and is darker in colour. Its high sulphur content has led to its being utilized in the manufacture of sulphuric acid: indeed in some acid solutions it is itself completely insoluble. Sometimes occurring with gold, Pyrite is a bright, silver-coloured, shiny mineral, formed in flat blocks with furrowed, straight lines on their faces. Its shape is so perfect that, when they see it for the first time, most people think this stone must have been sculptured by the hand of man. Its name comes from the Greek *pyr*, meaning 'Fire', because of the sparks Pyrite gives off when subjected to friction.

Both Pyrite and Marcasite have a measured hardness of 6, Venus's own number.

Second Half Taurus (3 May–19 May): Bedside Rock

Irish Fairy Stone
Second half Taureans have a Venus-ruled, Saturn-mutable influence in their horoscope and are therefore entitled to this admirable mixture of cubic, blue-grey galena (the principal ore of lead), sparkling, clear rock crystal (the 'seeing Eye' of fortune tellers), yellow and black metallic Sphalerite (the principal source of many rare metals and the most important ore of zinc), and brassy little blocks of 'Fool's Gold', or Pyrite which together form the Irish Fairy Stone. As Irish as its name, here is a truly unpredictable gem in which not one of the crystals comprising it is what it originally set out to be.

The elements composing them started deep in Earth's crust as a conglomerate of dark rock mixtures. Then came pressures from deeper down still, in consequence of which these basic rocks were folded, broken, squeezed and melted, liquefied and re-hardened many, many times, on each occasion undergoing transformation into a completely new mineral. Finally they came to rest near enough to the Earth's surface, far enough away from the volcanic disturbances not to melt again, and ready to be discovered by man.

Such is the history of the Irish Fairy Stone, with its glittering mass of crystals displaying proud and dark splendour after their rough ride through time.

First Half Gemini (20 May–4 June): Precious Crystal

Orange Sapphire (Padparadjah)
In parallel to the bravest globe in our solar system, the steeliest crystal next to a Diamond insists on furnace-like conditions at birth. Belonging to the corundrum family, which derived its name from Kuruwinda, the Sanskrit for Ruby, the Orange Sapphire has an age-old reputation as the badge of truth, constancy and virtue. It exhibits a tone, transparency and tint which gained the corundrum clan a status as flowers among gems, since glorious shades are habitual. What causes the group's enormous colour range is nature's secret, except for the red, which is tinted by metallic chromium, and the blue, containing a whisper of titanium and iron. Although some of the softer hues have possible titles, only three popular names are geologically accepted. 'Ruby' for red, 'Sapphire' for blue and all other shades except orange which is called 'Padparadjah' (pronounced Padpa Radjah) or 'Orange Sapphire'. This name derives from the Indian, meaning 'Lotus Blossom', the Indians also consecrating this precious crystal to their goddess Lalita, better known as the Sapphire Devi of Fertility.

Pure corundrum is composed of oxygen and aluminium. But as colourless specimens are exceedingly rare, it is the vibrant and sumptuous shades induced by impurities that fetch the huge prices. What causes these tints it is impossible to ascertain, but this is an advantage in matching them with celestial bodies – the colouring agents are inimitable, and so, by definition, genuine. Indeed, as none of the chemicals are strong enough to be differentiated, the Padparadjah can be regarded as almost a perfect corundrum, which corresponds with Mercury by its great density.

Mercury's nearest planetary neighbour, Venus, with its orange-lit soil, is the mutable body in this part of the zodiac and is constantly threatened with sulphuric rain, so again the

Padparadjah qualifies by its immunity to acids. In sympathy with the most Sun-abused world in the solar system, the Padparadjah is resilient and will not fuse under tremendous heat, its lustre is enduring, and the fire in its being splits light into almost as many colours as the Sun produces. It also has a hardness count only one below that of the Diamond – nine out of ten.

In the corundrum family three tints in one crystal is a frequent occurrence, and this phenomenon is beautifully displayed in a much celebrated statue of Confucius, carved from a three-colour stone. It shows a transparent, white head, pale-blue body, and yellow-orange limbs.

Finally, imitating its heavenly partner's pulverized rock-dust surface, corundrum of poor quality has been used for centuries as an industrial abrasive. The ancient Chinese fitted bows with emery-covered cords (emery is corundrum dust) to shape other substances.

Taafeite is one of the rarest crystals known to man and gives a second choice to Geminis in the first half. Discovered along with other spinels by Count Taafe in 1945, Taafeite is almost as hard as a Sapphire and about the same bodyweight. It is a brilliant gem but, like the colourless Sapphire, almost impossible to obtain.

Second Half Gemini (5 June–20 June): Precious Crystal

Cat's Eye
The Greeks called it *Cymophane*, meaning 'Waving Light', but we know the precious crystal for part two Geminis as 'Cat's Eye'. This especially valued, translucent gemstone may have a golden-yellow, mid-yellow, bamboo-green or bluish-brown body, but whatever the tint, a powerful silver-white beam of light moves across its half-round or cabachon-cut surface when stimulated by even the slightest movement.

Known as a 'stone-gourmet's delight', this gem was believed by the ancients to guard against physical danger and the devil's assault against the soul. Its main characteristic, a bright ribbon of light, occurs through reflection of light from fine, paralleled fibres or hollow crystal tubes which the growing crystal encased when forming. Cat's Eyes are generally thought to be the most beautiful of the 'ray' gems and (unfortunately for those born under Gemini Two) are priced accordingly.

If a person in this group would prefer a transparent crystal, then the same variety of mineral to which the Cat's Eye belongs, known as the Chrysoberyl, will provide a brightness superior to most other gemstones. Seventeenth and eighteenth century Spanish and Portuguese jewellers favoured the Brazilian pale-yellow type, but the Gemini could have a rare colourless stone from Burma, or choose from yellow, brown, light-green, mid-green or deep bottle-green stones from, among other places, Burma, Madagascar, Zimbabwe, Russia or Sri Lanka.

The name Chrysoberyl comes from the Greek word for 'gold'. It has a superior brilliance, a hardness count of 8·5, and contains the metallic elements aluminium and beryllium and, sometimes, a trace of iron, all links with planet Mercury. Its bodyweight and rarer elements correspond, however, with Uranus, the mutable globe in this area of the zodiac.

First Half Gemini (20 May–4 June): Talisman

Moss Agate and Mocha Stones

Through the ages, men thought they identified, in the markings in Moss Agate and Mocha Stones, species of imprisoned moss, leaves and hairy plants. But what scientists not so long ago were still labelling as fossil remains was nature's blueprint for future foliage, for these two stones came into being long before Earth's present vegetation began to form.

Moss Agate and Mocha Stones are now known to be a quartz mineral compound comprising amorphous crystalline grains impregnated by natural, metallic fluids rich in iron and manganese. The interwoven patterns occurred when watery substances injected themselves or filtered into the cellular structure of the quartz. The iron and manganese fluids are commonly called 'green earth' and are formed in the cooling process of molten volcanic rock. Moss Agate has dark-green and blackish-green designs imitative of ferns and moss, while Mocha Stones have red, brown or black tree and plant patterns.

The Mocha variety was originally found near an Arabian seaport somewhere in the vicinity of Mocha and Moss Agate was first discovered in western India, the area which supplies some of the best specimens even today, including one of the largest examples weighing in at over thirteen and a half kilogrammes, or approximately thirty pounds. America's Rocky Mountains have an abundance of Moss Agate, the stream-beds there yielding fine quality material.

When still thought of as a stone incorporating fossils, Moss Agate was the chief talisman for farmers and agriculturalists, its main use being as an aid to water divining. At that time it was placed under the rule of planet Venus, as were all semi-transparent minerals with fossil-like inclusions, in tribute to Venus the goddess of fertility. Now both Moss Agate and Mocha Stones are seen as perfect parallels with planet Mercury (Gemini's ruler) and Venus (mutable planet in this area of the zodiac), particularly the former, since Mercury, scorched by the Sun, is so largely composed of metallic elements.

Another talisman for first set Geminis is the Uvarovite Garnet, which ranges in colour from transparent emerald to dark emerald-green. Primarily a calcium-iron crystal, Uvarovite is a new gem recycled by mother nature from 'old rocks' buried deep in Earth's crust aeons ago.

Second Half Gemini (5 June–20 June): Talisman

Transvaal Jade
Grossularia, the Latin word for 'Gooseberry', is where the second set Gemini talisman derives its proper, geological name, but the gemstone is better known as Transvaal Jade.

People who think of garnets as clear, red stones are in for a surprise, as Transvaal Jade is a garnet which is opaque and, at its best, bright green, but it simulates Mercury's blazing day by fluorescing dazzling orange-yellow under X-ray. Because all members of the garnet family originated millions of years ago, subjected in the depths of the earth to the vaporization and recycling brought about by volcanic action, they all contain a little of most metals and are weather resistant. But in each type of garnet one or two metallic elements predominate, and in the case of Transvaal Jade they are the white metals, calcium and aluminium. Chromium, a brilliant, white metal of industrial importance, has properties which impart hardness to iron and steel, and this element is responsible for the talisman's green hue. A pink version is coloured by manganese, a pinky-grey metal which is also used for toughening steel. Transvaal Jade always contains some iron, but some varieties have black flecks contributed by a magnetic mineral called magnetite.

The less vibrant examples of Transvaal Jade come from Burma, Canada and Scotland, but the brightest and best quality occurs in Africa, whence eggs and wonderful jade carvings of creatures and human heads can be obtained, as well as the occasional bit of jewellery.

Mercury is the globe with the largest metallic core in the solar system, and in this area of the zodiac Geminians' mutable planet is Uranus, the big, green planet well endowed with metallic elements.

Varieties of the transparent grossular garnet family are alternative choices for Geminians of this set: for instance, the gem quality green crystal type to which vanadium provides its tint, the yellow variety, which fluoresces orange and the clear white type, a lovely gem but hard to obtain.

First Half Gemini (20 May–4 June): Bedside Rock

Staurolite
This stone derives its name from the Greek word *staurus*, meaning 'cross', and is naturally cruciform, with a notable iron content which makes it an obvious match for planet Mercury and a resilience which suits Venus. In colour it is usually a vibrant red or grey-brown but very occasionally transparent Staurolite crystals are found which, when cut and polished, resemble 'table-wine garnets'. In laboratory tests some varieties of the gem fuse, changing under stress into a black, magnetic glass – a recognized feature on planet Mercury's surface.

The ancient Britons called these gems 'fairy stones' and used them in magical rites. The early Christians knew them as 'cross stones' and wore them as lucky charms, while myths speak of 'Staurolite stars' falling from heaven.

A second bedside rock for Geminians here is Verdite, which hails from the Transvaal. A noted fertility stone, it was administered in powdered form by witch doctors to barren women. This brilliant, opaque and ornamental member of the serpentine family stands apart from its cousins by virtue of an added ingredient – the glorious, green fuchsite mica, much utilized in the electrical industry. The metallic elements magnesium and iron are usually present in Verdite, which occurs in lumps which make it a popular stone for carving. Lions, frogs, hippopotami, owls and all sorts of other animals are produced by African craftsmen and sold in commercial shapes.

Second Half Gemini (5 June–20 June): Bedside Rock

Rubellite in Lepidolite

Formed in excessively hot, pressurized conditions, this small piece of fluffy iridescence comes in a variety of hues – rose-red, pink-violet, violet-grey, lilac, grey, and yellow-white colourings which it owes to industrially important metallic chemicals. Lithium, used in batteries, medicine and ceramics, is one; aluminium is another. Then there is mica, which is used as a thermal insulator, and last but not least, potassium. Rubellite comprises many metallic and non-metallic elements and when found in gem quality is a prized crystal. The metallic elements in both Rubellite and Lepidolite ensure correspondence of these minerals with planet Mercury, while their light bodyweight and water content supply the link with Uranus. They occur in pegmatites, which are veins of mixed minerals formed in the final stages of volcanic cooling.

A second bedside rock for part two Geminians is the Geode or Potato Stone. This mineral product of an old volcanic bubble is of roundish proportions. Its outside is solid agate, its centre is beautified by lacy Rock Crystal, Amethyst or Opal, a conjunction brought about by the watery, mineral-rich fluids which percolated into the cavity or hole left by the bubble which occurred in the lava when it was steaming hot. The outside of most Geodes is coated with a fine film of Green Earth, or Delessite, caused by iron and magnesium-rich fluids running and squeezing their way through all the cracks and splits which were not filled with the more solid minerals.

Rock shops generally sell Geodes in half pieces (either matching pairs or singles), but Geminis must have both halves, as their emblem is the Twins. Some inventive jewellers set mini-Geodes in silver and gold to be worn as cufflinks, earrings, pendants and pins. The main sources of Geode supply are Brazil,

Mexico and South America. The part two Gemini mutable planet (Uranus) balances the water content of the Geode.

First Half Cancer (21 June–4 July): Precious Crystal

Adularia

Probably the most precious variety of Moonstone, Adularia echoes the Moon's pearly sheen. It has a soft, luminescent glow in striking contrast to the flared radiance of most precious stones. When cut in domed shapes a hovering line of light dances across its surface giving the illusion of being above the crystal, rather than coming from the fine, fibrous particles within. Named after its place of discovery in Adula, Switzerland, the gorgeous Adularia is nature's purest version of the simple field rock known as Feldspar.

This pale blue-mauve gemstone was once thought to have medicinal powers which triumphed over epilepsy and was considered a cure for love-sick women. Another ancient belief was that if an Adularia was held in the mouth it would cause the memory to quicken. Beads of Adularia were carried in the pocket to ensure potent good fortune and Gypsy races believed that during the Moon's waning period the Adularia was the best stone to use in foretelling future events.

This Moonstone is sensitive to pressure and is formed at low temperatures making it an ideal match for the Cancerian first half mutable planet (Pluto) and its satellite (Charon), since both are on the outer limits of the solar system, while its composition tallies with the most prolific minerals found on our Moon, which is the Cancerian ruling body. Australia, Burma, Brazil, India, Sri Lanka and Tanzania are the most important sources of Adularia.

Another precious crystal for first half Cancerians is Cat's Eye Scapolite, which occurs in the romantic shades of transparent to translucent pearly pink, violet, yellow-pink, yellow and white. Rarely cut as a gemstone as it was only discovered in 1913 in Upper Burma, Scapolite contains aluminium, calcium and sodium. The last two of these, being water enticed, correlate with the Moon by virtue of its effect on Earth's water. Aluminium relates to the moon because it remains untarnished by air (an element absent on that satellite). Cat's Eye Scapolite is always cut cabachon (half round) and occurs in Madagascar and Tasmania as well as those countries already mentioned.

Second Half Cancer (5 July–21 July): Precious Gem

Water Opal

Of the beautiful Opal, Pliny the Elder ecstatically wrote: 'It is made up of all the glories of the most precious gems and to describe it is a matter of inexpressible difficulty'. Even more could this be said of its variant, the Water Opal, in whose crystal-clear depths the colours dance through the spectrum like bubbles riding on a dolphin. Its basic tints of electric blue and grass-green intermingle with violet flames, behind which flares a pink trail reminiscent of camp fires in the continent mainly associated with this stone, that is, Australia. The Greek compiler Onomacritus, writing four hundred years before Pliny, conceived the Opal as having the tenderness and colour of a beautiful child's love. That too could be said of the Water Opal.

Because of its unique combination of pattern and hue, an Opal can never be duplicated. Geologically, it is classed as a quartz, the world's most abundant mineral, and indeed Opal and quartz occur together and their chemical composition is almost identical. But here the likeness ends, for quartz has a three-dimensional character while Opal is a glass-like material composed of spheres so small as to be invisible to the naked eye. These spheres, or cells of silica, must be of uniform size to give first-class quality and pattern. Yet it is not the spheres themselves which produce the Opal's unique loveliness but the refraction of light on the material packed between them. Top quality Water Opal comes from an area in south Australia called Andamooka.

On their surface, the rarest white Opals have what looks like a hovering star. This phenomenon, known as asterism, is caused by fault areas or breaks in the regular pattern system of the cells. As Opals contain more water than other gems, and accordingly will shrink and expand with changes of temperature, they must be set with longer claws than any other gemstone or otherwise held in for safety. Their high water content makes them parallel to the moon and to the mutable planet (Neptune) now established scientifically as having the same density as water.

First Half Cancer (21 June–4 July): Talisman

Pearl

Cancerians are lucky to be able to claim as their talisman a jewel with such a long, well-charted and distinguished history. Four thousand years ago a word denoting 'Pearl' was recorded in a Chinese dictionary. Caskets dating from Ptolemaic times have been found with Pearls still inside them. In Byzantium Pearls were used to adorn crucifixes and prayer books and, on one occasion, a box containing a relic of the True Cross; and they featured just as significantly in the religious history of Christian Rome. Pearls have been hoarded by pirates, dived for in the South Seas, and treasured by many princes, among them England's Henry VIII and Elizabeth I, as well as by the tragic young Lady Jane Grey, queen for nine days, who wore a single Pearl drop on a cross up to the eve of her premature death. Pearls, in fact, have been a sign of distinction both sacred and profane. Does not the Book of Revelation inform us that each of the gates of the Heavenly City is crowned by a Pearl?

Being formed in water, the Pearl is an apt talisman for first Cancerians whose ruler, the Moon, regulates the waters of Earth, and it also parallels Charon, the main satellite of Pluto, these Cancerians' mutable body. Mother-of-Pearl and Snail Shells are other talismans for people in this area of the zodiac.

A true mineral talisman for Cancerians (for Pearls, being organically formed, fall into a different category) is Rose Quartz, thought to owe its tint to the metallic element titanium, of which the Moon has a plentiful store. Like the Moon, this stone gives off light almost as generously as it receives it. In laboratory tests it shows traces of lime, water and manganese, elements all suitably gentle for the lunar world. Its mid-rose can fade to pale pink on exposure to heat, but the former colours will be restored if the stone is thoroughly soaked in water.

Rose Quartz is less common than most other variations of quartz and only top grade has the necessary gem clarity. The most beautiful and unusual species features a four-pointed star, which moves around its surface according to the play of light.

Called Star Rose Quartz, it is best cut cabachon (half round) and to dream of it is said to herald peace in one's domestic affairs.

Second Half Cancer (5 July–21 July): Talisman

Red Coral

The Greeks believed that sea-nymphs stole Medusa's severed head and that the drops of blood seeded Red Coral. The Romans thought that if their youngsters wore twigs of vivid Coral round their necks they would be safe from danger. Indeed, some Italians even today wear Coral for protection against the Evil Eye. They also prescribe it as a cure for women afflicted with sterility. The Gauls ornamented their weapons of war with the brightest Coral twigs available and Coral was once worn by Chinese Mandarins to signify their high position in government service.

Geologically speaking, the Cancerian talisman is a hard substance comprised of the lime secreted by whole tribes of marine animals for purposes of shelter. A coral reef is simply a mass of such protective structures, the ocean's answer to a housing estate.

First recorded in 1712 as a plant growing at the bottom of the sea with neither seed nor bloom, and embellished with pores like stars, this gemstone is still fashionable as a gift for new-born babies, having once been considered the cure par excellence for teething troubles and bad tummies in growing children. Indian astrologers rated this sea-flower highly, commending it in all its shades to anyone cursed with a badly aspected Saturn. They also, wrongly, considered Red Coral to be the appropriate stone for Arians, whereas in fact it is not Mars but the Moon which must be matched with this watery gem of organic origin. Neptune, however, gets a look-in too, exerting its influence by virtue of being the only planet to have the same density as water.

First Half Cancer (21 June–4 July): Bedside Rock

Aragonite and Calcite
Calcium minerals of ethereal fragility should grace a first set Cancerian's home as his or her bedside rock, and Aragonite and Calcite of the land variety, formed in dry lake beds or in hot springs, are the two first choices. A lot of Calcite was originally Aragonite, which turns into Calcite under pressure of its own weight. Coral, for instance, is Aragonite on the top and Calcite at the base. Weighing a little more than Calcite because of its water content, Aragonite changes to Calcite or crumbles when exposed to a hot flame.

Although both Aragonite and Calcite are normally translucent, there is an absolutely clear variety of Calcite called Iceland Spar which, when placed over a line drawn on paper, will produce a double image, due to the splitting of the light into two rays. A particularly attractive type of Calcite is Flos Ferri, a luminous, snowy and tree-like variety with branches often sprinkled with iron fragments which cause a pinkish, though patchy, coloration. Other impurities may lend tints of grey, blue, green, violet or yellow. Nailhead, another variety, resembles a bunch of nails as its name suggests, and Dogtooth Calcite, equally obviously, has the appearance of canine teeth. Calcite is the basis for marble, chalk and limestone, and is a common constituent of fossil shells.

Other bedside rocks for Cancerians of this set include any colour Coral or even a cluster of barnacles, which sometimes have a surprise fan of Coral hiding in a cup.

The Moon is very obviously the celestial ruler of these minerals formed in water-orientated, gentle conditions which equally suit the planet Pluto.

Second Half Cancer (5 July–21 July): Bedside Rock

Desert Rose
We must thank the dusty Sahara for the loveliest form of this charming flower of the desert, which is formed through the percolating action of salt water evaporating from almost dry lakes. The water's movement picks up time-eroded granules of sand, coats them with a mineral substance and rolls them up

with similar grains which cling to each other to form tiny rounds of matter projecting exterior shelves or fine wings. As the percolating water and weather conditions continue their work, these materials group together and the result is a Desert Rose. Obviously this stone contains quite a lot of water which evaporates in heat, when – lo and behold! – this poetic-looking jewel turns into prosaic powder and becomes . . . plaster of Paris! The Bedouin believed that the Desert Rose was created from the tears of their womenfolk mourning for lost warriors – but that was a long time ago. Desert Rose belongs to the gypsum family of minerals and can be grey, buff, reddish, pale-yellowish and brown.

As a bonus for second half Cancerians, an alternative bedside rock is another precious crystal called Selenite, which is fragile and must be cherished. Selenite is transparent, tinted grey, yellow or brownish and always exquisite. Like the Desert Rose it should never be washed in soapy water, which wrecks the lustre and leaves an unattractive opalescent film. Nor indeed should any form of gypsum be soaked in liquids. Instead, and only if it really needs cleaning, sweep the stone with a soft make-up brush or in clear water and dry quickly.

Yet another bedside rock for this area of the zodiac is Enhydrous, a stone commonly known as a Water Nodule. This amazing creation started life in a cavity left by a volcanic bubble or a decomposed shellfish. In time this void became encrusted with the form of quartz known as Agate and inside this, in a bath of trapped, mineral-rich water, grew the rock crystals. If part of the Water Nodule is sliced and removed, the pre-historic water can be seen swishing around its hiding place and the weight of the water felt when held in the hand. Brazil and the Western coast of America yield most Water Nodules.

First Half Leo (22 July–5 August): Precious Crystal

The Yellow Diamond
This stone can be cut in countless styles from the modern round 'brilliant' with 58 facets and the appearance of a spider's web when viewed from above to the 25-faceted 'full Dutch rose'. Equally, this stone may come as a simple 'rough', either polished

and shiny in its natural state or alternatively 'sugar-frosted', having been 'sprinkled' by another mineral.

A Diamond is actually a pure crystal of carbon which started life deep in the earth many thousands of years ago. The carbon, dislodged from its ledge by volcanic disturbances, mingled with molten rock and made its way under pressure along cracks and fissures towards Earth's surface. Then more volcanic action probably occurred and the whole process repeated itself: break, fold, remelt and rise and each time new minerals were formed. The carbon became a Diamond and settled in a rocky mix of soil called 'Blue Earth', along with Pyrope Garnets, Olivines, shiny flakes of Mica and a few other gems formed under similar pressure and heat.

No wonder the Diamond is the hardest substance known to man, with a top count of ten to match the Sun's given number. Its name is derived from the Greek word *adamas* meaning 'Invincible', its structure is ultra-complex, and its atomic composition is held together by powerful bonding.

This stone is appropriate as first half Leo's precious crystal because Jupiter, the mutable influence on the sign at this point, seems, when viewed from Earth, to give off a yellow light. There is also thought to be a degree of radiation emanating from Jupiter, as well as from the Sun (Leo's ruling galactic body), and the yellow Diamond, in the opinion of gemmologists, is probably coloured by radiation.

Second Half Leo (6 August–21 August): Precious Crystal

The White Diamond
Sometimes this flawless gem is referred to as 'of the first water', meaning a Diamond of the purest kind. Traded by Indian merchants in the fourth century, it was called by them 'a fragment of eternity', and from Indian mythology comes the legend of the Koh-i-Noor, which came to mankind on the forehead of the child Karna, son of the Sun and of a princess of the reigning family. Legend decreed that only a god or woman would be exempt from punishment and injury as a consequence of possessing this stone, and tragedy indeed stalked 'the Mountain of Light' where it was kept before being seized and, in 1850, presented to Queen Victoria. Since then it has adorned the

crown of state worn by three other royal ladies – Queen Alexandra, Queen Mary and the present Queen Mother. But, significantly, Britain's four most recent kings have all chosen *not* to wear it, so perhaps its terrors still hold. It is now in the Tower of London.

The ancients believed that the White Diamond would protect them from harm – anyone plotting against the owner of such a stone would have his evil designs catapulted back at him. For unhappy Leos with lunatic tendencies, the traditional cure was an elixir of water, alcohol and Diamond dust – this, however, is supposed to have brought about the untimely end of Emperor Frederick the Second.

This stone is well chosen because the Diamond is the Sun's own crystal, and also because Mars, the mutable planet in this area of the zodiac, has been observed to have its soil coated with a thin layer of white.

First Half Leo (22 July–5 August): Talisman

Zircon

The gem-loving Greeks were so besotted by this stone that they named it after a favourite flower, the Hyacinth, while the Persians called it Zargun, meaning 'all shades of yellow'. For centuries, deep in the Cambodian jungles, where most of the ravishing specimens occur, the natives heat-treated the more prolific orange-brown Zircon until its colour changed to a glorious sky-blue, a process which is carried on today in Thailand. In either shade, its brilliance is often equal to that of a Diamond. To Catholics this stone once signified humility, while Hindus associated it with the sacred kalpa tree. In ancient lore it was thought of as a guard against poison. Its allocation to Leo comes through Jupiter, the mutable body for Leos in the first half, with which it is thought to share certain scientific properties. It is variously named, according to its tints. Zircon itself denotes green; the yellow variety is called Jargon, the orange Jacinth, the brown Malacom, and the clear, or white, is Matura, name of the famous temple site.

In 1833 geologists discovered a stone which has become a second talisman for part one Leos, namely Phenacite. Originally mistaken for Rock Crystal, it is harder and heavier than that mineral, with a brilliance and play of light approaching that of the diamond. Taking its name from *phenas*, the Greek word for a deceiver, Phenacite comes in shades of pale rose, wine-yellow and clear white. It is found in Brazil, Mexico, Namibia, Zimbabwe, Russia, America, Switzerland and Tanzania, and contains the rare metallic element beryllium.

Second Half Leo (6 August–21 August): Talisman

Heliodor
For second set Leos, there is a talisman of golden-hued Heliodor from South-West Africa. This crystal belongs with the beryl family as does the Emerald and Aquamarine, but neither of those two could be coupled with the Sun as only the Heliodor is thought by scientists to be radioactive.

The Heliodor is conceived through and born in extreme pressure and high temperatures. It has a light bodyweight and an uncommonly high melting point. The intensity of its hue is thought to be caused by iron, the same metallic element that is responsible for the rusty-pink Martian soil (Mars being the mutable planet for second set Leo).

Another Talisman for second-half Leos is the very lovely yellow or green Sphene. The Sun's pure white light comprises the full spectrum of the rainbow and in correspondence Sphene contains titanium, a metal which lends the full spectrum to other metals when applied as a surface coating. Titanium is also a metal of unsurpassed toughness and will not melt in the most elevated temperatures. For the mutable planet, Sphene contains iron. At gem quality it also possesses qualities of light fit for a Sun-ruled individual, while corresponding suitably with the frosty, white surface of Mars. If your jeweller can't supply this glorious gemstone, it would be well worth a trip to Switzerland, America, Brazil or Mexico, where it mainly occurs.

First Half Leo (22 July–5 August): Bedside Rock

Vanadinite

Sun-ruled Leos in the first group, with Jupiter as a mutable globe, have this brilliant orange-red or dazzling yellow-brown mineral as their very out-of-the-ordinary bedside rock. Belonging to the lead family, and rich in vanadium, a grey metallic element used for strengthening steel, Vanadinite comprises unusual, complex chemicals and only begins melting in exaggerated temperatures.

Our Sun is a heavenly furnace of radiation, and Jupiter, albeit to a lesser degree, generates that same energy. When ice mantling the body of Io (Jupiter's principal moon) melted, its water vaporized into space and ultimately produced the golden haloes potent with radiation which even now continue to crown it, while its red and yellow colouring results from active volcanoes. Nature presents Vanadinite in all tints of amber, yellow, orange-red and ruby-red, not a hue out of place as a match for either the celestial sovereign or the mutable body. Gloriously pretty, tougher than steel, and sometimes holding minute amounts of arsenic, Vanadinite crystals usually grow on dark, weathered-looking rock, luxuriously filling crevices and coating the outside with smaller, lighter coloured and sunset-toned crystals.

A second rock for first-half Leos is Muscovite, which contains mica. An occasional Diamond may be found where mica resides because together they were formed in and migrated from deeper earth, travelling along nooks and crannies until close to the surface. Usually Muscovite is flaky. Sometimes, however, it develops in long, flat sheaves resembling a row of silver-backed books.

Muscovite derives its name from 'Muscovy' (the old name for Russia) which led to the same word being employed to denote other temperature-resistant products such as furnace doors and windows. Now Muscovite is used as an electrical insulator and a host of other things including artificial Christmas 'snow'. This pearly, shimmering mineral also contains aluminium and iron, both elements emanating from the Sun. Placed against the light, Muscovite shows up as a six-pointed star and appears in translucent shades of grey, yellow, brownish, green and white. This part one Leonine bedside rock is an abundant mineral, with America, Canada, India and Russia being its primary producers.

Second Half Leo (6 August–21 August): Bedside Rock

Sulphur
Known in Biblical times as brimstone, this rock is usually found
perched on a dark, parent rock and is generally formed in
translucent, box-like crystals of bright yellow, some measuring
several centimetres across. When a sulphur crystal is held in the
warm palm it will expand, and when rubbed will produce a
negative charge. Sometimes Sulphur occurs in column-form, or
in tiny, powdery lumps. It is not always pure and added chemicals will give the basically yellow mineral greenish or amber
tones when lit from behind. A nest of Sulphur crystals becomes
a gorgeous mass of luminosity, a ravishing centrepiece for any
Leo home.

Homer refers to Sulphur as incense, probably owing to a
confusion with roll Sulphur, which is obtained by melting and
casting unrefined forms of Sulphur into thin sticks which burn
with a blue flame. Roll Sulphur was used for many centuries as
a purging agent after illnesses, as a means of cleaning out a
dwelling infested with bugs, and in the hope of driving away
demons. It was also applied to insect bites.

Today Sulphur is a major constituent in gunpowder, matches,
fireworks, fertilizers and fungicides and has an annual production of over 24 million tons worldwide. America (one state
alone produces three million tons a year), Canada, France, Italy,
Japan, Mexico and Russia are among the suppliers. To parallel
with the Sun, Sulphur forms through hydrogen-based chemical
reactions and in conjunction with Mars (the mutable planet
here).

Other bedside rocks for second half Leos are stones known
as 'Volcanic Bombs'. These resemble small, blackish pears and,
while not pretty, are certainly fascinating. Measuring only a few
millimetres in diameter, Volcanic Bombs originate as molten
rock spewed out from a volcano. While still fluid (or plastic)
these pellets spun in flight, and in the process gradually solidified
into spindle-shaped, solid minerals.

First Half Virgo (22 August–5 September): Precious Gem

Black Opal

Until recently the only Black Opals in the world came from a nine-square-mile area in New South Wales, Australia, called Lightning Ridge. Now top grade stones have been discovered in Indonesia, where they cost less because their potential market value is less well understood. Both occurrences yield a semi-black Opal as well, but the Indonesian Java Black, with its flashing, irridescent 'fire' – a range of colours covering the whole spectrum and set off against an absolutely jet-black background – is a particularly appealing gem and more than suitable for this area of the zodiac.

The subtle stacking of a once liquid mineral gel to form layers of uniform, spherical cells accounts for the depth and vitality of this exquisite gem, with its rainbow-like colours formed by a refraction of white light.

The only Black Opals in history are those the Romans had an insatiable desire for. They came from Hungary and are now believed to have been poor quality White Opals artificially coloured by having sugar or honey burnt into them. It is important that Virgoan people understand that a top calibre, solid Black Opal is meant, not a doublet or triplet, pretty as these may be. The 'triplet' is a thin slice of Opal glued to a dark background and topped with a transparent dome. The 'doublet' is the same, minus the clear crown, although in rare cases it can be a slice of Opal capped with another, clearer material, or a natural doublet of the boulder variety.

The ancients believed the Opal was the mineral bridge between heaven and earth, for which reason they sometimes called it 'The Eye of the Universe'. Even more significantly it was, and is, 'The Stone of Hope'.

Second Half Virgo (6 September–21 September): Precious Crystal

Iolite

This crystal's composition of two white and two dark metallic elements corresponds with the dark side of Mercury, which popular astrology says rules the Virgo personality, and equally with the sun-bleached side of that planet.

Deriving its name from the Greek word meaning 'violet', Iolite's display of different tints when viewed from different angles also earned it a nickname – 'dichroic'. Most gem quality Iolite grows in empty cavities originally made by gas bubbles in hot lava flows. Matching Mercury's intensely hot position and its mutable planet (Venus), Iolite is formed under pressure and in elevated temperatures, where concentrated steam and rare metallic chemicals force their way through lava already cooling to the last solidifying stage in the centre mass. There, in empty spaces, some of the mineral-rich liquid hardens into large, perfect Iolite crystals, containing varied mixtures of magnesium, aluminium, iron and manganese.

In times past Iolite was known as 'The Water Sapphire'. It is iron that gives it its prevailing blue-violet shade, although unusually lovely specimens from Sri Lanka show interesting red hues, caused by added iron mineral scales within the body of the stone, which is then called bloodshot Iolite.

Alamandine Garnet, sometimes called Carbuncle when cut cabachon (half-round), is another precious crystal for second half Virgos. All Garnets have the same basic composition, formed at elevated temperatures, and all are rich in metals, though these differ with each variety. The Alamandine is predominantly an iron/aluminium composition and, when cut as a Carbuncle, the most famous member of the Garnet family. The ancient Greeks, wizards with the drill and cutting wheel, worked on it to good effect as a fashionable stone, and their artistry lives on in a Carbuncle carved about the middle of the sixth century BC. On its surface, carved in exquisite detail, a man wearing a cap, draped in a cloak and seated on a rock, is offering a cup to an eagle as large as himself. An arched, leafed tree encircles both and a further line denotes the flat earth.

Crusaders carried Carbuncles as a protective agent against battle wounds. Just as 'working Diamonds' are used in the manufacture of machinery, so imperfect Garnets are found in stones used as building blocks.

Another Virgoan Red Garnet, called the Arizona, or the New Mexico Ruby, was once gathered by the Navajo Indians from ant hills and scorpions' nests.

First Half Virgo (22 August–5 September): Talisman

Labradorite
Due to the presence within this mineral of countless minute iron plates, Labradorite shimmers in iridescent shades of peacock-blue, green, gold and greenish-yellow. Sometimes a pinky-red or purple specimen peeps shyly from its hiding place. Like a dragonfly's wings and with true Mercurian swiftness the colours appear, then vanish, this optical effect being achieved, in the main, by interference of light in Labradorite's physical structure.

The background tint of this, the loveliest variety of feldspar (Swedish for field rock), is often deep-grey, while a more ethereal type is a transparent pale grey, but whatever version Labradorite presents itself in, it is Mercury-ruled (like the people in this area of the zodiac) with Saturnian undertones, Saturn being the mutable planet for first half Virgoans.

Used through the ages for cameos and carvings, Labradorite nowadays is mostly cut flat for mounting in rings or in circular shapes for beads. But nothing delights connoisseurs of this mineral's gentle grace so much as a simple string of tumbled, drilled, natural Labradorite stones. It should be mentioned here that a pure, crystal variety Labradorite has recently been discovered in Australia, but lacks all the beauty and fascination of the non-gem-quality stone.

The mausoleum constructed in Moscow in the 1930s in order to house the body of Lenin is built of red Ukranian granite and Labradorite – tons and tons of it, probably from pits in the Urals. The stone itself is named after the country in which it was first discovered, namely Labrador.

Another talisman suitable for Virgos of the first half is the Spessartine Garnet. Jewellers use five members of this family in the course of their work, corresponding to the number (5) allotted to planet Mercury by the science of numerology. Its hardness and metallic constituents make this a definite Virgo talisman. It occurs in America, Brazil, Africa and Sri Lanka.

Second Half Virgo (6 September–21 September): Talisman

Tiger's Eye
Resembling the gleaming eye of a tiger in the night, this stone has a golden streak of light which stretches full width across its curved and polished surface, giving it a shifting lustre. Fashioned in beads, it presents parallel, pale, silk-like ribbons of colour alongside deeper-tinted velvety bands, wheeling and reversing its colour order with each movement. An iridescent combination of yellow-brown and chocolate-brown is the shade generally associated with the Virgo talisman, yet Tiger's Eye can display variegated greens alongside bronze-red or it can have lemon-tinted lines revolving round (and beside) dark-blue.

Its geological name is crocidolite, which also denotes the fibrous asbestos mineral which, infiltrating its basic quartz body, can give it an indigo-blue tint. Less glamorously, crocidolite is used for brake linings, boiler coverings, fire-proof fabrics and insulation. There lies the correspondence to Mercury (Virgoan ruling planet) and Venus (mutable body). By natural process in Earth's crust, crocidolite changes composition (not form) and usually assumes a yellow-brown tint, which makes it the more commonly seen yellow Tiger's Eye, but sometimes a part-way mark is reached in the change process and a residual portion of the original blue product produces green Tiger's Eye, or 'Zebra' to the trade. If there has been no change to the crocidolite, the gemstone remains dark-blue and then it is termed 'Hawk's Eye'. The red Tiger's Eye is another matter altogether as this shade comes from re-heating, which can happen naturally in the earth or artificially at the hands of man. Tiger's Eye contains a trace of iron and was thought by the ancients to be a guard against the Evil Eye.

Blue-tinted Vesuvian Lava can hardly be called a gem, but is certainly a sterling second talisman for second set Virgoans. This natural, transparent enamel looks more than terrific when shaped and polished. When volcanic eruptions occur they cause fusion of minerals and after the molten mass has set, some areas glitter with a myriad of crystals, while others are dull. Most lava is unworkable by man, but the Vesuvian variety has most of the qualities essentially needed by craftsmen, plus an amazing tint and known history.

First Half Virgo (22 August–5 September): Bedside Rock

Specular Hematite

This glittering, black stone is one of the chief iron ores, which gives correspondence to Mercury's enormous metallic core and rock composition, while its colour links it to Saturn (the mutable globe in this area of the zodiac).

Hematite is an abundant mineral which often occurs in small crystals which, eventually, other minerals grow round and enclose. At other times it sprinkles itself on an already developed, separate mineral. Either way it then acts as a colouring agent to otherwise dull material. Although its own shade is a dark steel-grey, if it is scored on a ceramic tile the resulting streak is red, hence its alternative (but seldom used) name, 'Bloodstone'.

Hematite can be a blaze of crystalline radiance, or come in thin plates grouped in rosettes in specimens from Alpine areas. The type of Hematite used in jewellery develops a bulbous, kidney structure known as 'Kidney Ore'. Cameos, beads, ring-stones and cufflinks in Hematite are a 'must' for the fashion conscious.

A second bedside rock for Virgoans is Magnetite, another important iron ore. This also is an abundant and widespread high temperature mineral which, when occurring in sulphide veins, is usually magnetic, and was used to make early compasses, when splinters of the mineral would be placed in buckets of water and painted with points marked North, South, East and West. For this reason seamen once wore iron crosses as a talisman. Although this form of Magnetite guided many sea-going vessels to safety, we read in 'Tales From the Arabian Nights' of passing ships' planks being wrenched from galleons by the force of the attraction which mountains of Magnetite had for the nails!

Magnetite is commonly called 'Lodestone' and its magnetic qualities are extensively used in industry and for the purpose of attaining polarity in alternative medicine. Of this mineral a scholar once said: 'Being carried about, the Lodestone should be wrapped in red cloth and stored in a dry place so as to retain its virtue of curing cramp and gout. The Lodestone will also make a man gracious in conversation.'

Often Magnetite occurs in a dull, dark lump but sometimes it adds beauty to violet Amethyst, rock crystal and mica.

Occasionally Magnetite's iron content, or some of it, is replaced by magnesium, aluminium and chromium, but it is still a Virgoan mineral, since all the replacement elements are metallic and suited to a sun-boiled ruling planet. Magnetite has a hardness count of 5·5, which is Mercury's own number.

Second Half Virgo (6 September–21 September): Bedside Rock

Meteorite
Corresponding with Mercury's dense, sun-baked surface, a Meteorite has a hard crust where many chemicals have become fused and clotted by heat and pressure. Science categorizes these as 'stony', 'stony-irons' and iron. The second set Virgoan's bedside rock, then, is the remains of a large mass of primitive matter from the solar system generally thought to have originated in the asteroid belt between Mars and Jupiter. When flung out of orbit the material would have been automatically drawn by gravitation towards the Sun, and by chance or pull reached our atmosphere, where it became white-hot and usually exploded. Those fragments reaching the Earth are known as meteorites.

A dagger hewn from the Virgoan bedside rock was found in Tutankhamun's tomb; and once, some years ago and also in Egypt, an iron meteorite killed a dog. In general, however, these objects have done little harm. Indeed, most are so tiny that nobody ever finds them.

Another bedside rock for Virgoans here is Obsidian, once more, appropriately, registering a hardness of five. In fact, Obsidian is not strictly speaking a mineral but natural glass once spewed from an erupting volcano. Favoured by ancient Mexican cultures, this material, which is usually black, contains white and grey markings which have given rise to such appropriately descriptive names as 'Snowflake', 'Flowering', and 'Apache Tears'. Another variety, called Mountain Mahogany, has orange-red and brown bands, caused by cavities present at its formation. Mexicans once thought these tinted bands neutralized negative magic.

Green Obsidian flies under the flag of Bottlestone and is equally suitable for Mercury's children.

First Half Libra (22 September–6 October): Precious Crystal

Spinel

This chameleon among jewels has a wider range of tints than
any other variety and is rarer than Ruby or Sapphire, with which
it is often found. Unlike them, it plummeted in popularity about
a century ago for a variety of reasons, all of them unjust. Until
that time, its history was dazzling. The Black Prince wore a
Spinel at the Battle of Crécy. That same gem now glows alongside the world's second largest Diamond in the English crown
of state. The British royal family also own an uncut Spinel
known as the Timor Ruby – a stone rendered unique by the fact
that the six previous owners have their names drilled into its
surface. More romantically and sadly, a Spinel danced at the
high point of the last Tsarina's pretty crown.

Spinels come in several colours and for Librans of the first
half the best, in reverse order, are: the clear variety or transparent
white; the blue, containing zinc; and the dark-green type known
as Ceyloite containing iron and a trace of chromium. This last
is to be preferred above the rest because it pleases not only
planet Venus, Libra's ruler, but also Uranus, the mutable planet.

Composed of the metallic elements magnesium and
aluminium, Spinels of different varieties come from Afghanistan,
Burma, Sri Lanka and Thailand. The gem's hardness is considerable at 7·5 to 8.

As a second precious crystal Librans in this area should choose
a White Topaz. Occurring in acid-induced rocks, this gem is
usually found in Australia, Brazil, Japan, Zimbabwe and the
Urals.

A third crystal of great beauty is gem-quality Kyanite, the
purest of all forms of bedside rock adopted for Librans.

Second Half Libra (7 October–22 October) Precious Crystal

Blue Sapphire

From the Middle Ages onwards the Greek name *sapphirus*,
meaning 'blue', was recognized as referring to the Blue Sapphire,
a crystal of gem quality belonging to the corundrum variety.
Since then all tints except red and orange are referred to as

Sapphires, but when we use that name we generally mean blue and that is the precious crystal for second half Librans.

The Sapphire has a basically aluminium composition and its colouring pigments are iron and titanium. It is a hard gem at a count of nine, is not attacked by acids and remains solid even when exposed to elevated temperatures. It is a worthy Earth mineral partner for the metallic worlds of Venus (ruling planet) and Mercury (mutable), both of which are exposed to the unimaginable heat of their close neighbour, the Sun. The blue and blackish tints are allotted on the grounds that most astrologers agree that Librans are influenced by the nights of their celestial monarchs, but these individuals may choose one of the brownish-blue or greenish-blue shades.

Probably the most desired, as well as the rarest, of the Blue Sapphire's tints is the intense cornflower colour with its velvety translucence. Called the 'Kashmir', this occurs in Burma and Sri Lanka, but earlier it came from the mountainous Kashmir region of India, a deposit now sadly worked out. Librans who find the Kashmir unobtainable or above their means should take a look at the Star Sapphire. They may find they forget the Kashmir when they watch in fascination their ruling planet's effigy mirrored in this wonderful six-rayed star.

A fine Star Sapphire is easy to define. It should have good colour (though Starstones are generally paler than clear crystals) and the star should be well centred on the stone and have straight, strong rays. 'The Star of India', at 536 carats, is the largest cut blue stone in existence, while the largest Black Star Sapphire is the 'Midnight Star' weighing 116 carats. The hypnotic black-bodied Starstone is also correct for this area of the zodiac. It occurs mainly in Australia.

Unlike the other Sapphires (which are facetted), the Starstone must be cut cabachon (that is, half-round) in order fully to display its six-rayed star, sometimes caused by inclusions of rutile (needle-like crystals) which run in three directions crossing at a common point. Rutile is a separate mineral which the growing Sapphire crystal trapped as it developed. In conjunction with Venus and Mercury, rutile is used in industry as a source of titanium.

Sillimanite also sits well with Librans of the second half as it is often conceived in elevated temperatures, which make it uncommonly resistant to chemicals, heat and stress. The Sillimanite crystal most suitable here appears, at first glance, to be violet-blue, but when viewed from a different angle changes to pale yellowish-grey.

First Half Libra (22 September–6 October): Talisman

Dioptase
From the Tsumeb Diamond mines in South West Africa, and the oxidation zones of copper deposits, comes a glittering cluster of hypnotic green crystals more vibrant than any Emerald. This is Dioptase. Yet though matching the brightness of its ruling planet's glimmer from Earth, this transparent gem has not yet emerged as suitable for cutting. An inherent brittleness has disqualified it to date, but pendants, earrings, cufflinks and bracelets are fashioned by leaving the gleaming Dioptase in its original uncut state and placing, or electroforming, metal on its base and sides. The result may be thought of as a gold or silver mount holding elfin dreams. Dioptase is right for this area of the zodiac, being rich in copper and usually found in association with sulphur, a main constituent of Venusian rain. It matches Uranus, the mutable planet for Librans of the first half, because of its colour.

A fashionable second talisman for Librans in the first half is Tsavorite. Belonging to the garnet family, this new, transparent, emerald-green to yellow-green gemstone was found in Kenya and introduced to the market by Tiffany & Co in 1974. It can withstand great heat and pressure.

Second Half Libra (7 October–22 October): Talisman

Imperial Green Jadeite
Green is one of the most sought after shades of the highly venerated Jadeite mineral and also one of the hardest to find. There are many other colours – white, red, rust, yellow and all shades of violet – but emerald-green is chosen for this area of the zodiac because that tint is due to chromium, which when added to iron and steel imparts hardness and tenacity, qualities

needed for an Earth mineral parallel to both Venus (ruling planet) and the mutable body, Mercury.

The Chinese call Jadeite 'Yu Shih' meaning the Yu stone. They believe it contains all five virtues needed for a happy and civilized existence; charity, courage, modesty, justice and wisdom. In times past the Chinese Emperor wore Jadeite sandals and his officials had badges of office of the same material. To this day great Jadeite boulders embedded in orange clay are cracked open by heat. Then, after being wedged apart with chisels, they are cut with thin, steel saws held tight on bamboo bows.

First Half Libra (22 September–6 October): Bedside Rock

Kyanite
Formed in stressful circumstances and containing aluminium, Kyanite is the perfect example of symmetrical elegance, and the bedside rock for first half Librans. Habitually reminiscent of greyish-blue sky, its finely furrowed, flat blades stretch tautly, reaching as far as its chemicals will allow, a soft luminosity glowing from its grey-blue depths showing lights of patchy-white, muted-green and pale-mustard.

Kyanite also occurs in rosettes, which still show its pearly lustre and shading to good advantage. It is remarkably heat resistant and is almost completely immune to the forces of other chemicals (such as acids). When heated to 1,300 degrees Centigrade, it not only decomposes into the aluminium-type product known as Mullite but also into silica-rich glass.

It matches the opposing traits of Venus and Uranus with contradictions of its own. Venus spins close to the Sun and is torrid, while chilly Uranus trudges slowly on the outer limits of the solar system. Kyanite similarly shows a Jekyll and Hyde character by being much softer lengthways than it is across. The Greeks spotted this and called the stone *Distbene* meaning 'dual strength'. The name itself is from another Greek word and refers to its overall colour, that is, 'blue'. It is nowadays obtainable in most countries in rock form, with St Gothard (Switzerland) and Arizona (USA) yielding fabulous gem quality crystals – which clever Librans, incidentally, could wear as a precious gem.

Nature wasn't in a hurry when it designed Wavellite, another bedside rock for first half Librans. Containing aluminium and iron, the crystals of this mineral are best described as white and brownish-yellow needles with striated faces, which can be stout or long. But more usually Wavellite forms in masses of radiating fibres which start from the same common point and span outwards, making flattish spheres up to half an inch in diameter reminiscent of silk wound tightly on a circular piece of cardboard. A mathematician among minerals, it occurs in the county of Cornwall in England and at Holly Springs, Pennsylvania, in the USA.

Second Half Libra (7 October–22 October): Bedside Rock

Adamite on Limonite

For a model of their bedside rock, second set Librans should take a dark-brown pudding basin, chop half the sides away so as to leave the base intact, and let it find its own standing position. Next they should throw spoonfuls of pinky-violet water-ice into the vessel, letting the globular masses fall where they will. Then they should take thin slices of melon and place them on one side of the bowl's interior and sprinkle the lot with green icing-sugar. That completed, they should stand back and look at their creation with half-shut eyes. What they will see will be Adamite on Limonite.

Water-ice is reminiscent of Adamite, a translucent copper, zinc and cobalt mineral. Similar to nickel in many ways, cobalt is a silvery-white metal used to make a deep-blue paint pigment. Copper is a major metallic substance used in the electrical and pharmaceutical industries, and zinc is employed in many fields necessary for man's comfort and pleasure, among them dyemaking.

Limonite is a stone containing a lot of iron, its existence resulting from other iron minerals which have been altered by weather conditions. It either forms in 'icicle' structures, as squashed spheres, or in long, furrowed, flattened pieces. Most often these occurrences are shiny, but they can also be dull. Lovely specimens of Adamite on Limonite come from Mopimi in Mexico, Cornwall in England and from Saxony, Russia and America.

Second half Librans can use a component of their other bedside rock, Ilmenite, to make white smoke for sky-writing, yet this stone itself is black. It is usually glossy, contains iron, sometimes more metallic elements, and is an important source of titanium. It occurs in flakes and grains, in broad, flat crystals or in a chunk. Heavy beach sands often contain the granular type, notably at Travencore, a seventeen mile beach in India, and at beaches in Australia and America. Inland deposits occur in Norway and Quebec, so fun Librans of the second set can simply have a bucket of black sand as their bedside rock.

First Half Scorpio (23 October–6 November): Precious Crystal

Ruby
In the beginning, according to ancient Burmese legend, there was a great serpent which laid three eggs. The first produced the King of Pagan, the second the Emperor of China, and the third a miraculous seed which sprouted Burmese Rubies. These last were thought to guarantee invincibility in battle if the owner of the stone inserted it into his flesh. A similar belief in the Ruby as a protective gem was held by the Ceylonese, who thought it formed itself from the Buddha's tears. In the Bible a Ruby is placed at God's command on the throat of Aaron, the elder brother of Moses, and is designated the most precious of the twelve gems first created in the world. In the 14th century it was apparently believed that the Ruby should be worn on the left hand side to secure its protective properties, which included turning black to warn the wearer of imminent danger and regaining its vibrant hue when he or she was out of harm's way. Interestingly, a Ruby of exquisite quality worn by Catherine of Aragon, Henry VIII's first wife, was reported to have lost its lustre and inner fire when she lay on her deathbed in 1536.

First grade Rubies, generally known as 'Pigeon's Blood', carry a hefty price tag which would sink a comparable Diamond to the bottom of the deepest ocean. The most important sources are Burma, Sri Lanka, Tanzania and Thailand, the best deposit being in the Magok, or Mogok, Valley of Upper Burma. For centuries women and children have crawled along the narrow pits, shafts and tunnels which run at a depth of several yards under the surface of this valley to bring up specimens which, when sorted, yield only one per cent gem quality. Large stones are rare, but the work brings its reward because it also produces a proportion of first-grade, 'Pigeon's Blood' stones, of a rich deep-red touched with blue. Sri Lanka produces a less valuable but still attractive gem with tints varying from light red to raspberry, some of which are found by panning the river sands and gravel. Recently found Tanzanian Rubies show a distinctive hue ranging from purple to brown-red, while those from Thailand have always been brown-red. Ruby deposits cover many parts of the world, but most are unsuitable for jewellery as they are opaque or of poor colour. These are powdered and used as an industrially important abrasive known as emery.

The cordundrum variety of mineral, to which Ruby belongs, is the hardest naturally occurring material next to a Diamond. This hardness underlines the Ruby's correspondence to planet Neptune, the mutable mass for this area of the zodiac and itself prolific in Diamonds, as we have seen. The Ruby corresponds with Pluto and Mars by its colour shift from red to green when certain laboratory tests are applied, and by the fact that it comprises chromium and iron (responsible for its tints) and much aluminium in its basic formula. The Ruby's hardness count of 9 corresponds with Mars's number.

Ruby derives its name from the Latin *rubens* meaning 'red'. Foreign inclusions in a Ruby fail to diminish its value, first because they indicate its source area and second, because the Ruby's shade is recognized as the all-important factor of a class gem.

The Star Ruby, also suitable for these Scorpios, has the same composition as a plain Ruby, with the addition of a multitude of foreign, hair-like crystals which introduce a silky sheen. When the stone is cut cabachon (half-round), these crystals, growing in three different directions, produce a six-rayed star which hovers over the surface when the gem is moved. This very desirable stone usually shows a more prominent asterism if the Ruby's basic body-colour is pale.

If another precious crystal is desired, try Benitoite, a rare titanium mineral found in San Benito, California, USA. Discovered about 1907 by Mr Hawkins and T. Edwin Sanders, this normally deepish-blue gem is similar to a Sapphire, but excels it in brilliance. Not long ago a glorious pink was reported. At a count of 6 Benitoite can be recommended as very usable 'dress' wear.

Second Half Scorpio (7 November–21 November): Precious Crystal

Rhodocrosite
The second half Scorpio precious crystal began its career just before the Second World War when a forgotten mine, once worked by ancient Mexicans for silver and copper during the 18th century, was reopened. Now 'Inca Rose' and 'Rosinca' are understandably popular for the pink delight which is properly called Rhodocrosite. This stone comprises calcium, magnesium and iron, is formed in gentle circumstances, and is hard enough to wear and enjoy as a dress jewel. Rhodocrosite equates with Pluto, Mars and the Moon by its toning, elements and hardness.

A location in South Africa's Kalahari Desert produces top grade Rhodocrosite gem-quality crystals in shades ranging from clear and bright sunset-pink to varied shades of rose, but Rhodocrosite can have a greenish tinge through added impurities. Unfortunately the original Mexican mine has failed to yield gem material, but it does supply the world with the very lovely semiprecious kind, which is characterized by lacy cream ribbons on its bright yet soft-pink background. In fact this semi-precious variety is popping up all over the world in North America, India, Hungary, Romania and Saxony.

A second precious crystal for Scorpios of this set is the Sri Lankan Alexandrite, which is really a colour-change Sapphire of slaty-blue-green (in sunlight) to purple (under artificial light). Iron and other metallic elements including vanadium are for Mars and the Moon, while the colours are for Pluto. Buyers should be warned always to obtain a note of guarantee supporting this gem's authenticity, for synthetic versions of it are frequent.

First Half Scorpio (23 October–6 November): Talisman

Blue John

Nero is said to have handed over the modern equivalent of £120,000 sterling for a vase made of it; Pliny the Elder sang its praises; the Pompeii excavations revealed two Blue John urns, proof that the Romans not only discovered and mined this mineral 2,000 years ago in their outlandish province of Britain, but also cherished it. Today wine goblets retail in Harrods of London for up to £2,500 sterling and the Queen personally owns at least one modern Blue John chalice. Blue John occurs in only one place – a hill situated about a mile from Castleton in the county of Derbyshire, England. This stone, the world's most exclusive fluorite, is distinguished from others by its undulating dark-blue and purple-red bands on a white or yellow-white background, making circular, lacy patterns round a central focal point in colours matching both Pluto and its moon, Charon.

Fossils of marine life which swam in underground streams some 330 million years ago, and pockets of green oil (thought to be derived from extinct ocean vegetation), are found where Blue John has developed, giving it a tie with the watery planet Neptune, the mutable globe in this area. The secretive character of Scorpio's heavenly ruler and the sumptuous Blue John run parallel, as the prized ornamental bands of the stone have long been a source of mystery as to their cause. Could it be iron, asphalt, bitumen or radiation from uranium? Nobody knows. Even the origin of the talisman's name is a mystery. Was it from France, where masterpieces were fashioned from it? The French could have called it *bleu-jaune* (blue-yellow). Or did the British lead miners name it Blue John to distinguish it from their own working material, nicknamed 'Black Jack'?

In size matching tiny Pluto, Blue John is naturally formed in small, round nodules and gentle conditions. Superb selections of inexpensive jewellery in silver and gold mounts are available in this material, as are eggs, bowls, urns and clocks.

A worthwhile adventure for Scorpios would be a trip along the illuminated half-mile of Derbyshire canal leading to a series of underground chambers adorned with cascades of multi-hued stalagmites (limestone columns), where subterranean veins of their stone can be seen as nature yields it.

Second Half Scorpio (7 November–21 November): Talisman

Amethyst

Caused by radiation effects on iron, the colour of Amethyst matches the Plutonian surface. In addition to that, it has usually formed in the remains of old lava bubbles with an outside coating of a super-rich iron substance. Iron is the metal which colours the Martian soil rusty-pink and that planet is a sub-influence on all Scorpios.

Although most quartz, the family to which Amethyst belongs, corresponds to Saturn, planet Pluto is of equally light body-weight and far enough from the Sun not to deny the presence of water. In Amethyst, added flecks of iron and golden rutile (foreign hairy crystals) are occasionally present, making an extra piece of magic in parallel. Few specimens hit the market, unfortunately, but when they do they are collectors' items. Earlier associations of this stone include Saturn (its vinous tint connecting it with Bacchus), Neptune (the Romans dedicated it to Neptune's month, February), Taurus (Venus), Jupiter and the Sun. Amethyst quartz was also confused with the Oriental Amethyst which is in fact a Sapphire.

One of the stories linking Amethyst with Bacchus is that he frightened an innocent maid who changed into a rock crystal through fear of him. The remorseful god sighed and as his wine-soaked breath touched the miserable girl her veins ran purple with the tint of the grape. From then on the gemstone showed pity to those over-indulging in wine and was said to prevent drunkenness. So the ancients quaffed from Amethyst goblets, hoping to remain sober and avoid the morning after effect.

Amethyst was a popular choice in Roman times when engraving was in vogue, made possible by new instruments such as drills and turning wheels. So Mark Antony's handsome features can still be gazed upon today, causing us to understand why he won an Egyptian queen's heart.

First Half Scorpio (23 October–6 November): Bedside Rock

Stibnite

The shadowy world of Pluto attracts Stibnite, a brittle, bluish-silver to lead-grey mineral of excessive vulnerability and some malleability, its personality expressed in straight radiating needles or flat rods, sometimes with criss-cross lines which are usually grouped in parallel.

Stibnite occurs in small specimens matching the petite planet Pluto, is visually pleasing and occasionally exhibits surface iridescence. When heated in charcoal it shows its dislike of high temperatures by leaving as a residue a crumbly, white encrustation. White is the colour of Pluto's moon, Charon, and the intense cold of this globe suits Stibnite's softness, which is measured at 2 out of 10 on the hardness scale. Gentle Mars, a sub-influence for first-half Scorpios, and Neptune, their mutable planet, both have a low temperature and lead placid lives. Mars is a planet in which the soil is rich in metallic elements.

Stibnite derives its name from the Latin *stibnium*, meaning Antimony – a tin-white, brittle metal. About five thousand years ago it was used as eye shadow – perhaps the first luxury use of a product of Earth.

For those Scorpios who prefer rather more glitter in their bedside rock there is always Crocoite. This mineral has very shiny, clear crystals of hyacinth-red which usually display themselves on a brown parent rock, allowing this stone, so proud of its high-born character, full scope for showing off. Its colours correspond with Mars and Neptune by virtue of the fact that in one laboratory test the red crystals turn green, and with Pluto because, in the course of another, they turn dark before reverting to their natural red brilliancy. Found in Tasmania, America, Brazil, the Philippines, Hungary, Romania and Siberia, Crocoite develops in the oxidized zone of lead deposits. Its importance rocketed when it was found to contain chromium.

Second Half Scorpio (7 November–21 November): Bedside Rock

Okenite
Open the palm of your hand and imagine a small cave resting on it. Peer into its depths and see minute and shimmering Rock Crystals hanging at various lengths from the ceiling with more scattering the floor, these last straining to grow just a little bit higher. Strewn at random over the starry carpeting imagine balls of pale-green mimosa (wattle to Australians and New Zealanders) coated in glittering, seed Rock Crystals, their confusion suggesting the aftermath of a goblin fight. Then imagine these green balls rolling as you move your hand, and as the light plays on the seed crystals. Just inside and against the outside of the small cave are fluffy, white trees and bushes, with no branches and, in the case of the trees, no trunk. Each tree is just a mass of long, straight hairs, their pompom appearance caused by hairy crystals starting from a common centre point, their miniscule weight pressing them slightly flat at the base.

You are looking at Okenite, a calcium mineral with a high water content and an even higher fragility rating – one push and Okenite is gone forever! The shapes, whiteness and enormous size of this stone, compared with its mineral companions, correspond with Pluto's moon, for its delicate body is only able to survive if placed far from the heat of the Sun.

For Neptune and Mars the correspondence is rather with Prehnite, of pale-green 'Mimosa' appearance, another calcium mineral which differs from Okenite in having added aluminium and less water. This is an ethereal gemstone when tumbled, cut and polished, and often has a pearly lustre. Though not always easy to find, Prehnite, in the form of beads, pendants and cufflinks, is well worth searching for.

Quartz, the most prolific, and probably also the most appreciated, of all varieties of Crystal, is formed in gentle circumstances and suitably matches all three worlds involved. This additional choice is much discussed elsewhere in this book, particularly in the healing section, and second half Scorpios are exceptionally lucky in this wonderfully useful and attractive bedside rock.

First Half Sagittarius (22 November–5 December): Precious Crystal

Tourmaline

There is only one precious crystal tempestuous enough to correspond with the wild world of Jupiter and that is the Tourmaline. The multicoloured variety known as Melonstone is allocated to first half Sagittarians, as usually it has a strawberry core surrounded by a blueish-green band, or a green-blue inside and an outer layer of pink. The pink is important as first half Sagittarians have the rusty-pink Mars as their mutable planet and the metallic elements causing the tint are formed in correspondingly cool temperatures. Although the green parallels with both Mars and Jupiter, in reality Tourmaline of any colour is correct for those ruled by this planet, in which many precious metallic elements are thought to be swirling about.

No other family of gemstones has the richness in colour variation of the Tourmaline, for the composition of each stone differs from that of the next and each tint depends on the dominant metallic element present when the crystal was formed. Like its ruling planet, the Tourmaline is extremely complex and often holds aluminium, boron, potassium, magnesium, iron, sodium and lithium in varying quantities in the one crystal – a point amusingly underlined by the English art critic John Ruskin in his book *The Ethics of the Dust* (1866), where he wrote: 'And on the whole, the chemistry of it is more like a mediaeval doctor's prescription than the making of a respectable mineral'. Indeed, the only regular feature of the Tourmaline is its basic structure – the variations thereafter are myriad.

The Tourmaline's unique positive and negative electrical properties gave it its early name of 'The mineral magnet'. Warmth also activates it, as a group of Dutch schoolchildren discovered in 1703 while playing in the Sun with what they thought were worthless stones. In fact these were coloured Tourmalines which had been given to the children by gem traders and which attracted dried leaves and twigs. Adults then took up the game, placing Tourmaline gemstones near the fire or rubbing them with their hands, whereupon they were found to entice ash at one end while repelling it at the other. This caused the Tourmaline to be nicknamed 'Aschentrekers', meaning 'drawer of ash'. The Tourmaline probably derived its name from the Tamil word Tormalli, meaning 'something little out of the earth'.

Most Tourmalines are small but exceptions to this are the famous 'Brazilian Rocket', measuring 109 cm (43 in), and the nest of variegated crystals as large as a man's head found in Burma and given by the King of Ava to the Count de Bouron. The separate crystals making up this cluster are almost as thick as a pinky finger and each starts at the base of the stone as a dark shade, becoming more luminous towards the extremity. Although most of the surface is golden-brown, the mass, as a whole, is a pale violet-red. The King of Ava's extravagant gift now lives in the British Museum. The collector can find Tourmalines in Australia, America, Brazil, India, Russia, Zimbabwe and elsewhere.

A second precious crystal for these Sagittarians is Phosphophylite from Bolivia. The delicate, turquoise tint of this transparent gem, which can be cut, polished and handled, echoes Jupiter's steady light as seen from afar, and one of its principal components, zinc (the other main ones are iron and manganese), matches Jupiter's white southern zone. With its low hardness of 3·5, it is perhaps best kept in a tiny box rather than worn as an ornament, but either way there is no worry. Amber, with a hardness of 2·5–3, has endured for centuries after having been handled, worn – and sat upon.

Second Half Sagittarius (6 December–20 December): Precious Crystal

Tourmaline
Already matching Jupiter, this stone is also in parallel to the Sun, which is the mutable body for second half Sagittarians, by virtue of its light bodyweight and astonishing energy.

The most suitable colours or predominance of colours in this powerful crystal for Sagittarians of the second set are the yellow-greens and the blue-greens, but as Tourmalines in one or even two colours are relatively rare, additional tints or even quite different ones are acceptable. In matching the Tourmaline and its celestial counterparts the key factors are the stone's compositional elements, its density and its energy output.

To connoisseurs, the most alluring quality of a Tourmaline

is its butterfly personality. Green will show anything from yellow to greenish-blue, red displays varied pinks, dark red and brown have mingled tints and the clear stone has shadings of rust and green glinting from some spot within its body. The violets merge with turquoise; yellow can be dark, light, or even orange. Sections of cut Tourmaline exhibit contrasting shades on opposite sides. In most Tourmalines, in short, the rainbow seems to be throwing a party.

The Tourmaline should be called 'The Gem of Youth' as it has almost always come to fame through children. For example, on an autumn day in 1820, two schoolboys from Mount Mica in Maine, USA, spotted a glittering mass of brilliant green crystals by the roots of a tree. From there the stone came to the notice of Parisian jewellers who used it extensively, although even now the Tourmaline is too 'new' to be used by the smartest shops for regular window displays.

Over the centuries this harlequin mineral has been confused with other precious crystals. Thus a 'Hen's Egg' Tourmaline was originally thought to be a Ruby of remarkable light, and a stone of this sort is housed in the treasure room at the Kremlin today. It was first presented to Kaiser Rudolph II (died 1612) by his sister; from him it passed to the Swedish Crown; and from there it became the property of Catherine the Great in 1777.

Tourmaline is found in many countries but an accessible place for finding one of your own is the island of Elba, which produces some of the loveliest in the world.

First Half Sagittarius (22 November–5 December): Talisman

Amber
One thing can be said with confidence about Amber: it is unlikely to exist on any planet except Earth. For this substance is not a mineral (though it can be cut and polished like one) but a fossil of vegetable origin which came into existence between 25 and 125 million years ago in the form of sap or resin from certain types of vegetation. This sap, as explained elsewhere in this book, made a honeyed crypt for all manner of prehistoric objects from orchids, feathers, drops of water and spiders' webs to ants, fleas, moths, hatching eggs and basking lizards. A particularly bizarre specimen, now in the possession of an American natural

history museum, is a lump of Amber containing three sets of copulating flies – a sort of Pompeii without the people.

Formed of carbon, hydrogen and oxygen, Amber is soluble in alcohol, scratches easily and has a negative electrical charge when friction is applied, hence its ancient name of Electron, the Greek for 'electric'.

Amber from Sicily often glows internally with rich-green and brown-red tints. That from the Dominican Republic does the same, if less vividly, but occasionally specimens display a bright royal blue which shows when placed in direct lighting. The softer, opaque, butter and honey-coloured Amber comes mostly from the Baltic area.

Amber was prized by prehistoric cultures, doubtless because it was easy to work and light to carry. It also appealed to them as Sun worshippers. Attempts have been made to identify it as a 'Peace Stone' but, oddly enough, it has usually become most popular in societies in the throes of political upheaval.

Because of its low melting point – one of the lowest of all gemstones – amber is suitably placed with Mars, the mutable planet in this area of the zodiac, which is covered with a constant ground-frost.

The Eilat or Elath Stone is a second Talisman for Sagittarians in this set. Legend has it that it first came from King Solomon's copper mines, and it is certainly rich in that mineral. It also includes Turquoise, the other half Sagittarian talisman. Its usual colouring is a rich blue-green, but it can also be found in a gorgeous pink variety. It is found near Eilat on the gulf of Aqaba on the Red Sea.

Second Half Sagittarius (6 December–20 December): Talisman

Turquoise
Once the most sought-after gemstone of antiquity, Turquoise represented not only beauty to the Egyptians, but perfume as well, for this jewel was originally fashioned into the shape of the leaves of the sweet-smelling lotus. Those early inhabitants of the Nile Valley concerned themselves very much with gardens. In their daily prayers they asked to be allowed to return from the 'Land of the Dead' to sit under the blue lotus tree, eat its fruit and bask in its sweet and heady scent. Party guests wore

garlands of lotus, boatmen wore a single bloom, and bowls of lotus flowers decorated the poorest homes and grandest palaces, while lines of single petals and buds were sculptured and painted in tombs.

The Egyptians' desire to give permanent form to all things beautiful led them to trade with their neighbours for Turquoise, and to develop the art of cloisonné jewellery originally fashioned in Ur. Making this jewellery was an exacting and exhausting task. First, fine sheets of beaten gold had to be cut to a required shape. Then wires were soldered round the detailed design. Finally, the resulting hollows were filled with Turquoise strips, imitating the long, curved petals of the lotus. The forget-me-not, another much admired flower, was imitated in the same way, using the left-over Turquoise pieces. To add the final touches after all the strips of Turquoise had been slotted into place, the surface of the jewel was brushed with tinted and powdered limestone and heated by flame until the gold and the gemstone were fused. Shoulder-buttons, clasps, pendants, crowns and many other pieces of beautiful cloisonné art-work survive in Egypt to this day.

Turquoise was also jewel royal to the kings of Persia, where the gemstone was thought to protect horses and their riders and featured accordingly in pieces designed for both. This ubiquitous talisman came to Europe from Persia via Turkey, hence its name. Wearers still use it as a guard against the Evil Eye, and to dream of it is said to foretell a new and lasting friendship.

American Indians thought the stone made a man warlike, and implacable towards his enemies. Thus the well-equipped brave would carry with him on a war party corn, sweetcorn, beans, dried meat, a bear-claw – and a chunk of Turquoise.

Turquoise contains water, iron, copper and aluminium, an appropriate combination for Jupiter. It is of medium hardness, light in weight and largely resistant even to a strong flame (though heat turns its colour brownish) – a durability which matches the Sun, the mutable celestial body in this area of the zodiac.

Turquoise for world-wide supply comes mostly from North America, but the buyer must make sure to obtain a certificate of guarantee if a fine stone is required, for the average specimen is an imperfect soft stone hardened up and improved by means of wax impregnation and tinting.

Fossil teeth and bones, coloured by components of iron, are often cut and polished, reaching the market as Bone Turquoise. These of course must also be distinguished from the genuine stone.

A second talisman for people whose birthday falls under the domain of Jupiter is Hauyne. This pretty and very wearable gemstone resembles a slightly opaque Aquamarine and occurs regularly around the world. German Rhineland Hauyne, glowing orange under ultra violet lighting, matches Jupiter's clouds and Io, its largest moon. Hauyne is not as well known as one might expect. Its translucent beauty comes from a mixture of elements in its composition – sodium, aluminium and calcium – which matches it with Jupiter as does also its light bodyweight.

First Half Sagittarius (22 November–5 December): Bedside Rock

Aurichalcite
Specimens of this stone, formed in tufted nests of straight, needle-like crystals which correspond with their ruling planet, make a delightful bedside rock for first half Sagittarians. Like Jupiter, Aurichalcite has a light bodyweight, and reflects that planet too in its composition of zinc and copper, the former white and volatile, the latter malleable, enduring, and reddish. With its delicate, transparent blue or green tints it is as stunning as its celestial sovereign, whether it has formed in solitude, or with others, or on a dark parent rock.

A second bedside rock for first half Sagittarians is Chrysocolla, a mountain-green or sky-blue opaque mineral with an enamel-like lustre which can be found in Australia, America, Bavaria, Chile, the Congo, England and Siberia. Though of varying hardness, it is an unusual and durable jewellery material, showing both its vibrant colours, green and blue in the same piece, or even in the tiniest bead. Some truly gorgeous specimens contain Opal and Rock Crystal; others are overall turquoise in appearance; others again, depending on the impurities, can have brown or black markings as well.

Chrysocolla is essentially a copper element mineral, but containing also variable amounts of silica and with many other metallic and non-metallic elements present as inclusions. It occurs in the county of Cornwall in England; in Adelaide, South Australia; and in Siberia, Chile, the USA and Katanga.

Second Half Sagittarius (6 December–20 December): Bedside Rock

Bornite and Chalcopyrite

Both Jupiter's clouds and Io's volcanoes are honoured in these two stones. Bornite's red-bronze surface leaves a yellow deposit of sulphur when heated in the laboratory and is a valuable ore of copper laced with elements of iron. Chalcopyrite is simpler though more brassy in appearance. Whether occurring separately or as a duo, both these stones form in big, gaudy, opaque pyramid-shaped crystals, though sometimes triangular crystals appear and sometimes both stones occur in microscopically small crystals on a separate, dark rock. Bornite's 'eye-of-the-feather' iridescence has given it the nickname of 'Peacock Ore', but neither stone is ordinarily used as a gem material. Treasure each in its natural state. The Sun, which is the mutable body for part two Sagittarians, is as well pleased to be matched with these two flamboyant stones as are Jupiter and Io. They come from most parts of the world including, in particular, Australia, Japan, Korea, Chile, Britain, Germany and Norway.

As an alternative, Sagittarians of this half can try the well-named Thunder Egg. The origin of these stones is still a mystery to geologists, though it was probably volcanic action. Some, on the outside, resemble concrete hot-cross buns. They are much fancied by collectors. Good stones, when cut in half, show a four or five pointed star pattern, with the tops touching the outer edges. The centre of the stone itself can have a hollowed-out form, filled with clear Rock Crystal, opaque grey and red-brown quartz, or precious Opal. America yields some splendid specimens of this stone, which also occurs in profusion in Australia, notably in the states of Queensland and Tasmania. Warring gods in Aboriginal myth threw these stones as missiles, a practice no longer to be recommended, however tempting.

First Half Capricorn (21 December–6 January): Precious Crystal

Topaz

'The golden Topaz reminds us of autumn leaves, and so is the birthstone for November'. Such ignorant remarks have dogged the study of astrological gems and been the cause of much confusion. This particular observation would be less obviously ridiculous if autumn in all countries fell in the same months, or if natal gemstones differed from place to place or from one side of the world to the other. In fact they do not. Your gem is the same, whether you live in Sydney or Timbuctoo.

First half Capricorns score any colour Topaz as their precious crystal. Nicknamed 'Diamond slave' because its larger specimens often replace Diamonds for purposes of display, the colourless Brazilian Topaz has a pure, fierce brilliance typical of the whole family, even the highly coloured varieties. It was perhaps this characteristic which encouraged the age-old belief that the pious were able to read their prayer books in the darkness of night by means of the brilliant light emitted by a Topaz and perhaps also the reason why knights on crusade were given a Topaz by their lady loves before setting out.

Containing aluminium, Topaz is almost unique in being one of the few first-rate crystals to contain fluorine, a non-metallic element of considerable industrial importance. This chemical, plus a small amount of water and its consequent beautiful range of hues including blue, green, pink, yellow, brown and white, correspond with planet Saturn, and its hardness count of eight gives this stone the same digit assigned to Saturn by the science of numerology.

For Venus, the mutable planet in this area of the zodiac with sulphuric rain in its atmosphere, Topaz is also a match, since it decomposes only slightly when contaminated by sulphuric acid; also it is conceived in elevated temperatures.

According to fable, the Topaz was discovered and named by some shipwrecked sailors awaiting rescue. The island on which they were stranded was difficult to locate as it was constantly surrounded by mist and fog. The sailors called both the gem and the island 'Topazos', meaning 'lost and found'.

The Royal crown of Portugal has a very grand Topaz weighing in at 1,680 carats. It displays magnificent transparency.

Many stones however are wrongly sold as Topaz, including Yellow Citrine, the bedside rock for first half Capricorns. The Blue-green variety is often confused with Aquamarine, and the white with Rock Crystal, white Sapphire and the white Diamond, the Topaz being rarer than all of them. Superior examples of Topaz are not easy to come by, nor are large or pink toned specimens. Modern stones sold as Rose Topaz are merely natural yellow stones artificially heated.

Topaz is of wide occurrence and can be found particularly in Australia, Brazil, Burma, Sri Lanka, Russia, Mexico, Nigeria and the USA.

Chondrolite, another of the rare Fluorine gems, is a second precious crystal for first group Capricorns and is mostly thought of merely as an unusual mineral for a collector's box. It deserves more extensive use, however, for its deep-red crystals are of great beauty and lustre, and its hardness count of six out of ten makes it perfectly possible to fashion this stone for dress-wear. Red variety Chondrolite comes from the Tilly Foster mine in Brewster, Putnam County, New York, but not to be despised are the rich yet soft honey-yellows found in Kafvetorp, Sweden.

Second Half Capricorn (7 January–19 January): Precious Crystal

Tanzanite

An extraordinary purple-blue gem with violet lights flashing from its depths, Tanzanite, discovered in Tanzania as recently as 1967, is still to become well-known. Of the lighter bodyweight group, which corresponds with planet Saturn, and just over medium hardness, Tanzanite holds a reasonable amount of water along with calcium and aluminium. Its amazing blue tint is thought to be due to a trace of vanadium, a silver-white metallic element used in the manufacture of special steels.

Sometimes this stone is heated to enhance the blue even more, a process which does not invalidate its position as a Capricorn precious crystal but does diminish its natural intensity, hypnotic though the effect may be in other ways.

Another precious gem for second set Capricorns is the Opal Pineapple. Contrary to what you may think, this is not a crys-tallized fruit but an Opal-filled Glauberite crystal which started forming about 70 million years ago. The Opal's fast-flashing, changeable colour patterns belong to Mercury, the swiftest world in our part of the Milky Way and mutable planet in this part of the zodiac. Its featherweight body corresponds with the lightest planet in the solar system, which in no way compromises Opal's high water content, since Saturn sits far from the Sun in space.

For Capricorns, the tints of their Opal Pineapple are important, since their celestial ruler's body is yellow, shaded with indigo, blue and violet. Its flashes of other tints are appropriate too, as the planet's circuiting hoops are multi-coloured. The background colour, however, must always be dark.

Of all Opal Pineapple specimens found, only about two per cent are top grade. A lesson in life could be learned from precious Opals as their characteristic tints and designs come from structure mistakes and changed paths.

First Half Capricorn (21 December–6 January): Talisman

Jet

The most frequent word used in the English language to describe something ravishingly dark is 'Jet'. Tennyson described a maiden's locks as jet black and Shakespeare referred to Jet as a jewel. This lustrous and velvety gemstone accords well with Capricorns of the first set, for its tint blends in with the deeper shadows seen on their celestial sovereign, Saturn, and its light construction and bodyweight are equally appropriate. In parallel with the mutable planet, Venus, Jet needs tremendous pressure when forming. This stone, 'the Agate of the ancients', derives its original name from a river in Asia Minor, but the world's finest quality Jet comes from Yorkshire in England.

At a period roughly assumed to be 1800 BC, Northern British early bronze-age jewellers were fashioning great lunar collars with zig-zag patterns of up to fifty jet beads to each necklace. These collars often accompanied their wearers to the grave, and although the surviving pieces preclude analysis of their detailed designs, it is clear that the patterns were made by hand gouging. Each piece had triangular terminals and toggles, spacers of different shapes, and elongated 'beans' with multiple holes. In later times the devout carried prayer counters made of this stone. Jet was favoured in the seventeenth century for memorial purposes and in the nineteenth century, on the death of Queen Victoria's beloved Prince Albert, Jet was worn at court for the next twenty-five years. Prussian peasants still carve boxes, baubles and toys from Jet, which they call 'Black Amber'.

Although Jet is slightly harder and heavier than Amber, the two stones show similarities. Both release their own pungent aroma when burnt, both crack if not cherished, both explode under high friction or when subjected to violent temperature changes, both have electrical properties when rubbed, and both originated from prehistoric trees and are thus not proper minerals. Unlike Amber, which is resin, Jet is actually driftwood which was compressed under great pressure after being subjected to chemical action in stagnant water. It is much more difficult to obtain than Amber, and there is less of it in the world.

The lustre of Jet can be destroyed by perfume and body acids but is usually restored by a brisk rub on a soft cloth impregnated with beeswax.

Capricorns in this set have another talisman, Lazulite – a superb, ornamental stone which should be much more widely used than it is. Containing elements of iron, aluminium and magnesium, sky-blue to azure-blue Lazulite has a hardness of just below 6 and is a main constituent of Lapis Lazuli, the second half Capricorn talisman. Wonderful specimens of Lazulite are found in America, Austria, Brazil and Sweden. It corresponds with planet Saturn in all ways and is a match for Venus by virtue of its metallic elements.

Second Half Capricorn (7 January–19 January): Talisman

Lapis Lazuli

In an isolated area at a site where thousands once lived, and twelve miles from the banks of the Euphrates, excited archaeologists a century ago identified the King of Kish (sometimes called 'Me Silim'), resting in a suit of exquisite wafer-thin gold armour. Suspended from his shoulder was a gold filigreed sheaf worked as finely as a spider's web and containing a ceremonial dagger, its hilt carved from a solid piece of Lapis Lazuli. Another grave contained the body of Queen Pu-Abi, still clad in her best coat of woven gold thread and adorned with nine long Lapis

Lazuli necklaces, and a mixed stone choker of Carnelian, gold and Lapis beads. Adding height to her small figure was an enormous black wig entwined with gold ribbon and topped by three open, bright yellow-gold flowers attached to a triple-fingered comb. Crowning all this were wreaths of sheet-gold beech leaves embellished with Lapis Lazuli. Her two gigantic, double-hooped gold earrings must have jingled against the finery as she was laid in peace, surrounded by 63 attendants ritually slain. They too wore Lapis Lazuli beads, and also in the tomb were Lapis eating utensils, toiletry bowls and a talisman depicting fish and land creatures.

So second half Capricorns inherit the most coveted rock since at least 3500 BC. The poor of that time, who could not afford this precious stone, came to the conclusion that Lapis Lazuli inspired devout contemplation, since the Priest-Astronomers also wore it. But in truth the rich-blue jewel with silver and gold tinted flecks represented the night sky and the far-off dwelling place of the gods, Enlil and Anu, believed to inhabit the Sirius System known to Ethiopians as 'The Lapis Lazuli House'. Not much further on in time the peasants of the Nile, no more able to afford Lapis Lazuli than their earlier counterparts along the Euphrates, believed it counterbalanced the ill effects of incest, for how else, they must have argued, could the incestuous Pharoahs, who used these jewels as a permanent adornment, retain their sanity?

Despite the stone's slightly unstable composition, commercial Lapis weighs in at about the same each time and has a hardness rating of about 6. It was early found in the mountainous north-eastern region of Afghanistan, which Marco Polo visited in 1271 to view it in its natural surroundings. The region still supplies a fine quality. Iran, formerly Persia, yields the best, but political reasons make it impossible to obtain this at present. It also occurs in Chile, Russia, America, Canada, Burma, Angola and Pakistan.

In colour, hardness and its constituent elements, Lapis Lazuli corresponds admirably to Saturn, the Capricornian ruling planet and mutable body, while its metallic elements are ideal for Venus.

First Half Capricorn (21 December–6 January): Bedside Rock

Stichtite
Robert Sticht, an Australian, discovered the first set Capricornian bedside rock in Tasmania in 1910. Lilac-hued Stichtite is opaque, has a waxy finish and is sometimes veined in dark, slaty green. A magnesium and chromium mineral which often contains iron, Stichtite can be cut and polished. Though too young to have a romantic past, it provides choice specimens which are fast appearing in collector's showcases. Canada logged a Stichtite finding in 1918, as, more recently, did South Africa and Algeria. Stichtite's tint, weight and water content are well paralleled with the Saturnian world, and its metallic elements are ideal for first set Capricorns' mutable planet, Venus.

Members of the Quartz family, in which the violence of Venus, all heat and pressure and change, and the docility of Saturn are happily reconciled, provide alternative choices of bedside rock for Capricorns of the first set. Brown Quartz, properly called Morion, can be as light as a whisper and as dark as a moonless night – both in the same stone. Its transparency, whatever its shade, contrasts with the virtual opacity of Smokey Quartz, a similar mineral also once extensively quarried in the Cairngorm Mountains of the Highlands of Scotland. Many a Highland laddie wore a 'Cairngorm' in his kilt, and many a Highland lassie wore a similar stone in her sash. Now the supply from that region has begun to run short, so Citrine and Amethyst from Brazil have arrived to fill the breach. (They have similarly replaced the exhausted supplies of Kerry Diamonds from Ireland.)

Orange-gold Citrine owes its tints to a trace of iron in its composition and to the process of natural reheating in the Earth's crust. But it too is now becoming rare and its position in the market place has been taken by burnt Amethyst. Fortunately for Capricorns, reheating suits their horoscope, so this orange-hued stone is a more than acceptable match. Constructing a stone of double or triple tints, composed of a combination of Citrine and Amethyst, or of Morion, Citrine and Amethyst, is a new and developing art, although occasionally multi-coloured Quartz occurs in nature.

Second Half Capricorn (7 January–19 January): Bedside Rock

Rock Crystal

Rock Crystal, the perfect form of Quartz, is more associated with magic than any other stone. The ancient Greeks believed it to be an invention of the gods, since they found it first in a cave in Thessaly near the foot of Mount Olympus, legendary entrance to Heaven. They thought of it as water frozen perpetually by the Immortals and called it *Krystallos*. The first foundation of the Heavenly City, revealed by St John the Divine, was of Jasper, another variety of Quartz; and of course crystal balls have been used for centuries by soothsayers and fortune-tellers, genuine and false.

Rock Crystal forms in David and Goliath sizes. Some grow to the height of a small telegraph pole, others remain as minute as a speck of dust. A beach of ivory-coloured sand is about 99 per cent Rock Crystals, and if it wasn't for flint, in which Rock Crystals are also present, Man would hardly have emerged to become the dominant species on Earth. The most prolific of our minerals, Rock Crystal has a unique atomic structure which allows it to grow in exact mirror images. It began as a deposit from mineral-rich water journeying through cracks and cavities in cooled lava, or as quartz ingredients floating above others to form the top-most level in veins of many minerals. There its glittering purity added lustre to all the rest.

For the jewellery-loving or egg and sphere collecting Capricorn, Venus' Hair or Flèche d'Amour ('Arrow of Love') is a compelling second choice. Its criss-crossing golden lines suggest the energy emitted by Saturn while its light recalls the brightness of planet Mercury. Properly named Rutilated Quartz, Venus' Hair is actually clear Rock Crystal with fine, hair-like 'needles' of golden and reddish hue, formed of metallic titanium, that fiery mineral, patterning it from within. Germany is probably the best source of supply for this not easily available jewel.

First Half Aquarius (20 January–3 February): Precious Crystal

Peridot

Have you ever heard of a stone with an identity problem? No? Then meet the Peridot. Sought after as early as 1500 BC, it figures in the Bible disguised as a Chrysolite, or so many people believe. Nowadays, of course, green spinels are sold as Chrysolites, a Russian green Garnet is retailed as a Peridot and the Peridot itself is known in some countries as the Evening Emerald. Oh, and this stone is also known as 'The Serpent Isle Crystal', or alternatively as the Zibirat, owing to the fact that the island on which it was found, Zibirat, now St John's, in the Red Sea, is, or was, snake-infested. Is everything quite clear?

Yet first half Aquarians are lucky in their precious crystal, which belongs to the olivine family and displays a charming range of greens, from the palest yellow-green, through bottle-green to the dramatic deep olive, the most sought after by collectors as well as the most appropriate for those born under this sign. This type has yellow lights blazing from its depths. It is completely transparent, though with a slightly oily surface. Its light bodyweight and lack of density suit Uranus, its ruling planet, as does the fact that it only melts at high temperatures. Its constituent elements of iron and magnesium harmonize with Mercury.

The Pharoahs considered the Peridot to be the property of their gods and slew the slaves who guarded these stones on Zibirat on completion of their duties. In Christian times the Crusaders plundered these stones, giving them to churches which still have a large treasury of them. Australia, Burma, Brazil, Hawaii, Mexico, Norway, South Africa and St John's are the chief sources.

Another precious crystal for first set Aquarians is Brazilianite (from Brazil and the USA), a bright yellow to yellowish-green gem discovered in 1944. It has aluminium in its composition, is very light, and occurs in rather large crystals in correspondence to its celestial sovereigns. Its colour and hardness (5 out of 10 on the scale) make a good match for Mercury.

Second Half Aquarius (4 February–18 February): Precious Crystal

Diopside

Some seven thousand years ago a mine was worked in the Badakshan district of the mountainous north-east area of Afghanistan. Its treasure was a beauteous rock with tints varying from greenish-blue to rich purple-blue called Lapis Lazuli, but the crystal Diopside, a constituent of Lapis, remained hidden for much longer. Occurring pure and unaccompanied in fine gem material in Siberia and the Diamond mines of Burma, this stone only started to make a real impact on the world when absolutely top grade specimens appeared in association with Rubies in the Hunza Valley of Pakistan.

As a planetary correspondence, the circumstances in which perfect Diopside is formed has little stress and elevated temperatures, allowing the growth of a flawless gemstone from condensed vapour of re-heated fluids. But true to its Aquarian character, the Uranus cum Saturnian mineral waited for its supreme moment. Then, in 1964, the most resplendent Diopside of all materialized, displaying a four-rayed hovering star with two sharp and two muted lines, hanging suspended over an almost opaque black-green to brownish-black body. Possibly the only top grade magnetic gemstone, Star Diopside contains needle-like crystals of an extra iron mineral, making it fractionally heavier than pure Diopside and a fraction harder. Astonishingly, Star Diopside has hit the market without revealing its birthplace, which learned gemmologists locate most probably in Southern India. Italy produces a plain, sombre-green crystal Diopside. So do Austria, Sri Lanka and Brazil. Yellowish-brown comes from Canada, bright green from America and Russia. Violet Diopside comes from Piedmont in Italy and is often called Violane.

Diopside's light bodyweight parallels with both Uranus and Saturn, with a slight change of stoutness depending on the amount of iron present. With magnesium, calcium, and sometimes chrome, as well as iron in its composition, it also accords well with the metal-rich planet Venus.

Aquarians of the second group have another precious crystal in gem quality Tugtupite, which derives its name from *tugtup* meaning 'Reindeer'. This pink stone was logged as recently as

1960, after having been found lodged in a semi-precious mineral exclusive to itself, and used extensively in Greenland for ornamentation purposes. Of good dresswear hardness, the 'Reindeer Stone' is also found in the USSR.

First Half Aquarius (20 January–3 February): Talisman

Aventurine
The Russian craftsman and designer Carl Fabergé devoted many hours of skill to the resplendent Aventurine and in the English royal collection many treasures also exist – notably a bowl with silver mounts, a goblet embellished with red gold and moonstones, a box decorated with a combination of rose (cut) diamonds, olivines and gold, a sparrow with rose (cut) diamond eyes and a lovable farmyard pig with ruby eyes – all carved from various shades of this stone, which has also been favoured by craftsmen in China, from ancient times until today.

Green, pink and sunset-tinted Aventurine is a unique member of the quartz family and owes its gold-spangled countenance to featherweight flakes of mica in its body. Mica, with its shiny surface and heat-resistant qualities, is an excellent match for both Mercury and Saturn, while its bodyweight and remarkable complexity of composition make it a parallel for Uranus.

A second talisman for first-half Aquarians is Onyx, a lightweight quartz variety mineral with black, white and bluish-grey bands, corresponding with the black Uranian rings and the lighter Saturnian bands. Aquarians are in good company with such a talisman, for this was the material used by the craftsmen of ancient Rome when they wished to display their skills with the drill and cutting wheel. Using the layers of banded Onyx, they sculpted three-dimensional cameos on such subjects as 'Victory', usually depicted as a winged maiden with floating hair borne along in a horse-drawn chariot. The manes of the thundering steeds, the chariot wheels, and the locks and tresses of the girl were carved in Onyx of different shades, miraculously capturing the melodramatic scene in terms of the basic elements of the solar system.

Second Half Aquarius (4 February–18 February): Talisman

Jade
Certain Indians once considered that two good slaves were
worth one pure Jade axehead, prized for its toughness and shine.
Earlier still, in a country now known as Singkiang, peasants
shortened their miserable lives stoking furnaces by day and
extinguishing them by night in order to crack open great boulders of Jade and Jadeite. All night their calloused and blistered
hands chiselled and hammered the minerals until chunks were
broken off. The precious cargo was then loaded and transported
by camel-train to its destination further east. There it was carved
for the use of the Emperor who wore Jade sandals and in death
had a wardrobe of Jade. In 1983 a Chinese archaeological dig
unearthed evidence to prove that in the second century AD the
Chinese Emperor Wen Di, ruler of the area now known as
Canton, dressed in a Jade suit. Thirty Jade discs, each more
than twelve inches in diameter, had been placed below and
above the body and the tomb itself contained over a thousand
Jade articles, including a horn-shaped cup made of Jade and
forty-three ritual swords carved with dragon and tiger effigies.
This was a typical imperial tomb of the period.

Today descendants of those poverty-stricken slaves have small
Jade carvings adorning their own mantelpieces and more often
than not wear Jade charms. But the quarries of Singkiang in
Burma are exhausted of Jade proper (only Jadeite remains) and
sixty to seventy per cent of the world's Jade supply now comes
from the mountains of North-West British Columbia, where
well-paid crews blast with dynamite and cut the boulders with
diamond-tipped, diesel-powered saws. Motor vehicles transport
the Jade to Vancouver and from there it is usually shipped to
China where it is carved and sold as 'Chinese Jade'. This British
Columbian Jade is reputedly the best in the world. It is tough,
gloriously translucent, cool, gentle to the touch and easy on the
eye, and comes in shades of green from medium to almost
black. Unfortunately, however, supplies are running out – it is
estimated that they will have no more than twenty-five to thirty
years to run if demand carries on at its present level.

Jade belongs to the Nephrite family and its crystal structure
and light bodyweight give it a correspondence with Uranus,
Saturn and Venus.

In 1981 Jade carvings were presented to the Western political leaders at the Economic Summit meeting as a token of unity. There was an eagle for President Reagan of America, a bear for Germany's Chancellor Helmut Schmidt and a Canadian Goose for Britain's Prime Minister Margaret Thatcher. Davis Wong was the artist.

A second talisman for Aquarians of the second set is gem quality Casiterite. Heavyweight planet Mercury will be well parallelled by its ultra-high density, strong light absorbency and tints of yellow, buff and buff-grey, while Saturn will respond to the colours, which are the basic shades of its body without its shadows. The hardness count and water content are also appropriate for Saturn and even more so for Uranus, the ruling world of this area of the zodiac.

When Casiterite is not in its perfect crystal form, the non-gem quality is the chief ore of tin, found in many countries and occurring most often in Bolivia, China, Indonesia, Malaysia and Russia.

First Half Aquarius (20 January–3 February): Bedside Rock

Wulfenite

In this area of the zodiac the most influential bodies are Uranus and Saturn, both of them being big, gaseous balloons of sparse mass and light bodyweight, while Mercury, the mutable globe, is by contrast small and heavily compressed, comprising all, or almost all, the metallic elements in existence. Gold, red and green are the predominant shades of these galactic firmaments, and Wulfenite, with its splendid hues, unusually low hardness count, metallic elements, colour-shifts in laboratory testing, and metallic yield when heated, corresponds to them perfectly.

The metal yielded is lead (a Mercury parallel), but sometimes nature contrives to substitute products more suitable for the planets Uranus and Saturn. But whatever the changes, a silvery-white metallic substance called molydenum always remains. This is alloyed with steel for the manufacture of high-speed tools which themselves correspond to the planets Mercury and Saturn (Mercury for its swiftness, toughness and metallic elements, Saturn for its zooming, ice-composed ring system). Correspondence with Uranus emerges through the laboratory test when the Wulfenite goes through colour-shifts of black, flecks of green and black, yellowish-green and dark-green, all Uranian shades.

Wulfenite is named after Father F. Wulfen, the minerologist who discovered it, and who in 1875 described it and furnished coloured pictures of its crystals. Since then even more magnificent specimens of transparent red, gold and orange have been located in America, while elsewhere olive-green and honey tints have surfaced. Characteristically Wulfenite's crystals are seldom concentrated, matching (by density) its celestial sovereigns.

Second Half Aquarius (4 February–18 February): Bedside Rock

Charoite
The eye takes in a sumptuous version of what looks like purple Lapis Lazuli, causing the beholder born under other signs to wish that he or she were an Aquarian of the second set, and thus entitled to this bedside rock. Charoite does not come in shiny crystals or on an innocent bed of snowy quartz. It is an opaque, lilac-streaked mineral comprising calcium and potassium; not much in heavy metallic elements here, thus ensuring correspondence with Uranus and Saturn. To parallel Venus, Charoite comprises some metallic chemicals and its cellular structure is often fused. A mini-mystery about this wonderful mineral is, how did such an awe-inspiring, rich and hypnotic creation manage to hide in the banks of the Charo River in Vatutsk, USSR, until the late 1970s?

Charoite is an expensive stone and not easy to come by. It is also less easy to buy in its rough state than fashioned into eggs or the occasional piece of jewellery (and too often, alas, Charoite jewellery is set with a woeful lack of expertise). The time of this monarch of the mineral kingdom is yet to come. When it does, Charoite will assuredly take its place beside the famous Lapis Lazuli.

As a second bedside rock for second half Aquarians, try a modern sculpture of naturally formed Torbenite crystals from the county of Cornwall in England. The square of Torbenite, transparent to translucent in appearance, and emerald-green to yellow-green in colour, sits gleaming in thin, brittle plates of opaque, scaly stone. Torbenite is associated with uranium minerals and is distinguished by radioactivity.

First Half Pisces (19 February—4 March): Precious Crystal

Diamond; Aquamarine

Those ruled by the sign of the Fish are in a special situation. Three moons influence them: Triton (moon of Neptune); Io (moon of Jupiter); and the moon of our Earth. All are strong characters and demand possibly the services not merely of one gemstone but of two. The green-blue Diamond is a must for Neptune, a planet well supplied with Diamonds, as has been mentioned, and wrapped round with a covering of water and gases which, seen from afar, transmit the appropriate pale, green-blue hue. Triton, too, produces this appealing shade and is also likely to have hatched crops of Diamonds, by reason of the fact that its escaping internal heat could have caused methane gas clouds to break down to carbon.

Aquamarine tallies with all three moons and with the planet Jupiter itself, thanks to its composition of aluminium, lithium, silica, water, soda and berylium. Triton, with its lunar-type crust and density, its Earth-type atmosphere, and its limpid Neptunian depths especially calls for this stone. So first-half Pisceans are lucky indeed in having two such beautiful gems.

Aquamarine has a hardness of 7 on the scale (just over Neptune's own number) and often occurs in giant crystals appropriate to the size of both its planetary monarchs. Ancient soothsayers scrutinized its lucid depths. Simple folk thought these stones were formed from the solidified tears of sea-sirens, who kept them in cabinets on the ocean bed. In Renaissance England no lady in love with a sailor would let him leave her without his blue amulet. Nowadays the Aquamarine is found chiefly in America, Brazil, India, Burma, Madagascar, Tanzania, Zimbabwe, Norway, Russia and Ireland.

Second Half Pisces (5 March–19 March): Precious Crystal

Kunzite

Discovered in America about 1900 and named after the noted minerologist Dr G. F. Kunz, pink-lilac to dark lilac-rose Kunzite draws admiration by its flawless transparency and high lustre. It has great sensitivity and is uniquely phosphorescent. When subjected to X-ray it glows with a strong yellow-red or orange colour which tones in with the cloud colouring and major moon of the Piscean sub-influence (Jupiter), then turns blue-green, the associated tint of both Jupiter and Neptune. On re-heating, the triumphant sorcerer hidden in this lovely gem's depths returns to its original hue, matching Jupiter's rouged areas and Pluto's lighter regions.

Kunzite shows yet another loyalty to its celestial sovereigns by displaying visible flares of a blue-tinged green when viewed from a side angle. For Neptune and Pluto it contains a smidgeon of water; and like both these and Jupiter it contains that rare element, the soft and silvery lithium as well as the most abundant of Earth's minerals, the rust-resisting aluminium.

Kunzite has a hardness of about 7 (Neptune's number also), and a specific gravity measurement of about 3 (Jupiter's number). In imitation of its mighty rulers, it grows crystals of enormous dimensions; one is on record as measuring 42 ft × 6 ft × 2 ft and weighing in at 65 tons!

Wherever the stunning Kunzite occurs, so does another Piscean precious crystal, Hiddenite. Named after A. E. Hidden, the superintendant of the mine where it was discovered in 1879, this stone is generally identified with Kunzite in its body and composition but has a trace of added chromium, grows in smaller crystals, and has a weaker fluorescence. It is often called the 'Lithia Emerald'.

Transparent Euclase is another choice for Pisceans in this grouping, a rare crystal of fragile appearance in tints of soft or greenish blue, or else colourless. Not frequently found and even less frequently cut for jewellery owing to its unsuitable structure, this brightly lustred gem has the bewitching charm of an Aquamarine. Euclase contains aluminium and the rare metallic element berylium. In correspondence with its heavenly monarchs, and like Kunzite and Hiddenite, it has Neptune's 7 for hardness, a bodyweight of just over Jupiter's number 3 and a proportion of water. It occurs in Austria, Bavaria, Brazil, India, Russia, Tanzania and Zaire.

First Half Pisces (19 February–4 March): Talisman

Smithsonite
This stone holds the soft tranquillity of the Moon, the mutable celestial body in this area of the zodiac. It contains calcium and magnesium, both silvery-white; cadmium which is bluish-white and so soft it can be cut with a knife; cobalt; copper; and sometimes a little iron – all elements which harmonize with the Piscean ruler, Neptune, its sub-influence, Jupiter, and the Moon. Significantly, too, it is an important ore of zinc, without doubt the artist's metal and for that reason right for this sunsign.

Nicknamed 'Dry-Bone' owing to its cellular structure, Smithsonite is also marketed under the name Bonamite and is a comparative newcomer to the market. It is found in America, Britain, East and South-West Africa, Greece, New Mexico, Sardinia and Spain. Smithsonite is for those who prefer chic to overstatement. It has an exquisite range of gentle tints passing from grey-blue to medium-green and soft yellow, all corresponding with Neptune, Jupiter and the Moon.

A particularly fine second talisman for first-half Pisceans is Satinspar, a translucent to opaque mineral reminiscent of milk-coloured raw silk. Corresponding colour-wise with the stark Southern zone of Jupiter, all but one of Neptune's thirteen moons and indeed with our own Moon, this gem belongs to the gypsum clan, a group of stones which are often formed from chemical action between shells and sulphuric acid released on the decay of other minerals (usually those containing iron). By the same token Satinspar parallels elements found on Triton. It occurs where volcanic vapours have shown reaction to limestone or in the basins of dried out lakes, rivers or other waters, here parallelling our Moon, the mutable mass for this area of the zodiac. This pearly-white gem, composed of long, hair-like crystals solidly attached to each other, contains water and calcium, two more reasons for it to be happy with the cooler, outer planets and quite wrong for any explosive correspondence with the Sun.

Second Half Pisces (5 March–19 March): Talisman

Chrysoprase
This ancient 'Symbol of Reward' (whether of good or bad deeds)
was placed in graves in pre-Iron-Age Japan and by the side of
the deified cat and the lion-headed goddess Bast in ancient
Egypt. It was worn by Roman thieves to achieve invisibility, by
Alexander the Great in his girdle, and by Jewish High Priests in
their breastplates, besides being nominated as one of the twelve
precious gems in the Holy City. Though there seems to be no
real clue as to where the ancients mined this flawless beauty, it
is known that the Romans called it *phrase*, meaning leek-green,
and that the Greek name *chrysos prasious* translates as 'golden
leek'. Its stunningly rich tints also made it exceptionally popular
in the early Victorian era in England – until the jet-black of
mourning swept all away on the untimely death of Prince Albert.

In cheerful shades of apple to lime green, Chrysoprase occurs
in the town of Marlborough Creek in Queensland, Australia,
and comes in almost equally fine quality and profusion from
California, Brazil, Russia and Tanzania. Coloured by nickel, it
belongs to the chalcedony family, a variety of quartz formed of
microscopically small crystals. The Piscean talisman corresponds with Neptune and Jupiter by its light bodyweight and
basic colouring. Pluto, the mutable planet in this area of the
zodiac, is also happy with its composition.

A second talisman for second half Pisceans is Blue Lace Agate.
Marketed in the form of semi-precious jewellery, ashtrays, eggs
and solitaire sets, this is a soft, sky-blue, opaque gemstone. It
flaunts its innocence in translucent, white lacy patterns, and is
altogether a delight.

First Half Pisces (19 February–4 March): Bedside Rock

Opalized Fossil
An Opalized Fossil is a cast left by a disintegrated object which
has part filled with quartz crystals and later acquired Opal for
added glory. It is found in the hot desert areas of Australia,
once a network of rivulets in which flourished marine creatures
similar to our oysters and mussels. When the water receded,
trapped creatures dug themselves into the silt, their remains

eventually becoming so many empty chambers scattered about in dry land. A few yielded precious Opals but most were mere fossil-shaped shells, with a thin surface layer of Opal, the interiors filled with opaque, greyish-white stone. Opalized Fossils come from the tapering, pointed bones of extinct cuttle-fish called Belamnites or from sea-snails, which seem oblivious to their metamorphoses but live on in movement of colour and have incomparable beauty in this final, precious form.

Fossil Wood is another variation, a magnificent example of ingenuity, with dreamy tints of Opal dancing along ridges left behind by the departed product. Opalized Fire Cones, from America's Virgin Valley, are another variation again.

Opal Fossils have been chosen for first-set Pisceans because they have a double water influence: their ruling planet, Neptune, has the same density as water, while their mutable mass, the Moon, controls the swell and depletion of water we call tides. Opal holds more water than any other mineral – from one to twenty-two per cent in the dull valueless kinds and from six to ten per cent in the more precious varieties. Most Opal holds a trace of iron, and minerals with this element have been found on our Moon and are definitely present on Triton. For Jupiter, a Piscean sub-influence, Opal is appropriate because of its body-weight and the energy it gives out through colour and pattern changes.

Second Half Pisces (5 March–19 March): Bedside Rock

Fluorite and Apophylite

Fluorite usually has a basic white body, but can be angelically coloured in the softest shades of pink, green, amethyst, yellow and blue. Occasionally deeper tints make a showing, but even these gleam with a saintly translucence in keeping with the mineral's innocent character. Frequently occurring and obtain-able almost anywhere, Fluorite is an ideal match for the Piscean ruling planet, being formed, like all members of the calcium group, in cool, watery places.

Fluorite is often found in limestone caverns and as a natural cement in sandstone. Its crystals usually grow in cubes and, when hardest and of best quality, are cut as gemstones. To Western connoisseurs, the alluring sunset-pink from Switzerland probably takes top marks for unsurpassed good looks, though the Chinese favour the blue tones when carving the magnificent pieces which seem, through their inner strength, to draw the viewer into their very depths. Under ultra-violet lighting Fluorite gives a glorious glow – hence the term 'Fluorescence'.

Apophylite, the other bedside rock for second-set Pisceans, is also a water-related calcium mineral. This pearlized, milky glory sometimes has suggestions of rust, yellow, green or grey in its cleavages, thus acquiring the appearance of a great white cloud floating above a fairy-tale castle. In the trade's official view this stone does not have cuttable crystals. Yet its crystals *are* often cut and are cherished by collectors. The ethereal, cloud-like version of Apophylite occurs mainly in India, but another magnificent Apophylite bedside rock comes from Mexico, which yields an amethyst variety touched with pink. In whatever form, it is rarely opaque but rather translucent to transparent.

Both Fluorite and Apophylite are adversely affected by heat, which makes a suitable parallel for planet Pluto. For Jupiter both are equally appropriate through their colours, extensive occurrence, and water content.

A final note for those born under Pisces: all Piscean birthstones can be set with Diamonds, which appear to proliferate on their ruling planet, Neptune, as already explained.

Sunsign	Ruling Mass	Approximate Dates	Mutable Body	Precious Crystal	Talisman	Bedside Rock
Aries	Mars	20 March/ 3 April	Sun	Pink Diamond, Pink Sapphire	Sunstone, Heliotrope (Bloodstone) Plasma, Jasper	Cinnabar, Dolomite, (Pearl Spar) Quartz
Aries	Mars	4 April/18 April	Jupiter	Alexandrite, Rhodonite	Bowenite, Carnelian (Sard)	Youngite, Ruby Zoisite
Taurus	Venus	19 April/2 May	Mercury	Emerald, Oriental Emerald (Green Sapphire)	Azurite, Malachite	Marcasite Dollar, Pyrite
Taurus	Venus	3 May/19 May	Saturn	Andalusite, Chiastolite, Sphalerite	Lavender Jadeite, Pyritized Ammonite	Irish Fairy Stone
Gemini	Mercury	20 May/4 June	Venus	Padparadjah, Taafite	Moss Agate, Uvarovite	Staurolite, Verdite
Gemini	Mercury	5 June/20 June	Uranus	Cat's Eye Chrysoberyl	Transvaal Jade, Grossular Garnet	Rubellite in Lepidolite, Geode (Potato Stone)
Cancer	Moon	21 June/4 July	Pluto	Adularia (Moonstone), Cat's Eye Scapolite	Pearl, Rose Quartz	Aragonite, Calcite, Coral
Cancer	Moon	5 July/21 July	Neptune	Water Opal	Coral	Desert Rose, Selenite, Water Nodule (Enhydrous)
Leo	Sun	22 July/ 5 August	Jupiter	Yellow Diamond	Zircon, Phenacite	Vanadinite, Muscovite
Leo	Sun	6 August/ 21 August	Mars	White Diamond	Heliodor, Sphene	Sulphur, 'Volcanic Bombs'

Sunsign	Ruling Mass	Approximate Dates	Mutable Body	Precious Crystal	Talisman	Bedside Rock
Virgo	Mercury	22 August/ 5 September	Saturn	Black Opal	Labradorite, Spessartine Garnet	Specular Hematite, Magnetite
Virgo	Mercury	6 September/ 21 September	Venus	Iolite, Carbuncle	Tiger's Eye, Vesuvian Lava	Meteorite, Obsidian
Libra	Venus	22 September/ 6 October	Uranus	Spinel, White Topaz, Kyanite	Dioptase, Tsavorite	Kyanite, Wavellite
Libra	Venus	7 October/ 22 October	Mercury	Blue Sapphire, Sillimanite	Green Jadeite	Adamite on Limonite, Ilmenite
Scorpio	Pluto/Mars	23 October/ 6 November	Neptune	Ruby, Benitoite	Blue John	Stibnite, Crocoite
Scorpio	Pluto/Mars	7 November/ 21 November	Moon	Rhodocrosite, Alexandrite	Amethyst	Okenite, Prehnite, Quartz
Sagittarius	Jupiter	22 November/ 5 December	Mars	Melonstone (Tourmaline), Phosphophylite	Amber, Eilat Stone	Aurichalcite, Chrysocolla
Sagittarius	Jupiter	6 December/ 20 December	Sun	Tourmaline	Turquoise, Hauyne	Bornite, Chalcopyrite, Thunder Egg
Capricorn	Saturn	21 December/ 6 January	Venus	Topaz, Chondrolite	Jet, Lazulite	Stichtite, Morion, Citrine, Amethyst
Capricorn	Saturn	7 January/ 19 January	Mercury	Tanzanite, Opal Pineapple	Lapis Lazuli	Rock Crystal, Venus' Hair
Aquarius	Uranus/ Saturn	20 January/ 3 February	Mercury	Peridot, Brazilianite	Aventurine, Onyx	Wulfenite
Aquarius	Uranus/ Saturn	4 February/ 18 February	Venus	Star Diopside, Tugtupite	Jade, Casiterite	Charoite, Torbenite
Pisces	Neptune/ Jupiter	19 February/ 4 March	Moon	Diamond, Aquamarine	Smithsonite, Satinspar	Opalized Fossil
Pisces	Neptune/ Jupiter	5 March/ 19 March	Pluto	Kunzite, Hiddenite, Euclase	Chrysoprase, Blue Lace Agate	Fluorite, Apophylite

PART THREE

Healing Stones

Healing Stones

This section consists of two parts. First, a note on how your health is affected by stones and crystals. This is followed by a list of the most important healing stones, individually described, this time with reference to their holistic rather than their astrological properties. This Chapter is followed by a glossary of ailments and their treatment, in which many other stones are included. The reader may like to refer back and forth between this and the preceding, astrological section, thereby enhancing the benefits to be derived from both.

Precious Health, Precious Stones

The root of all illness is poison through imbalance. Holistic treatment is based on the theory that disturbances of the parts disease the whole. So what is required, and what natural healing provides, is a treatment for the whole body – or rather, for the whole person. It does not confine itself to patching up individual organs, as orthodox medicine is too often compelled to do. Of course the latter is frequently required – a broken bone cannot be repaired by rubbing it with a crystal. Ideally, orthodox and alternative medicine should be combined. The result would be a noticeable fall in the use of drugs and a faster recovery rate, with few or no side-effects.

There is one more requirement, however – self-help. 'Physician, heal thyself' is a good maxim for all of us, and there are countless ways, well publicized nowadays, in which we can hope to ward off ill-health and in the process achieve balance and happiness. We can take exercise, breathe and stand correctly, lay off tobacco and drink, even take barefoot walks along secluded sandy beaches letting the silicon work into our bodies from the undersides of our feet. Obviously, it is pointless to call in counsel from outside until we have determined to make the effort to help ourselves.

Unfortunately, few people seem to have grasped this basic fact. The average person turns to natural medicine only after all else has failed, and after years of punishing and ignorant abuse of his or her long-suffering body. Thus the crystal practitioner has to deal with destruction caused by drugs, the ravages of time and much else, as well as the ailment immediately apparent. Fortunately, holistic healers are seldom materialistic. They are ready to devote many hours to each patient's welfare, unlike orthodox doctors who are forced by necessity to book in the sick at quarter hour (or shorter) intervals, hand them a prescription, and send them on their way. Thus holistic methods can bring about healing at the deeper levels where the illness originated.

The previous section, on jewels of the zodiac, indicated the connections between particular stones and the astrological planets and signs, thus showing how we can improve our lives by living more closely in harmony with the universe. That in itself is a major contribution to health. This part of the book goes further. It describes the active, healing properties of stones, how we can use them to help ourselves and how healers can help us through them. How does this happen?

All healing is a transfer of energy from one source to another. A natural healer seems to transmit energy, in some mysterious way, from or through his or her own person to another human being. Sometimes the transfer is from plants to man or from man to plants. Often man benefits through the will of an animal. Pets, looking fondly at their masters or mistresses when they are ill, are wishing them well, and so healing them. Modern research bears this out. The work of the Crawford Centre in Melbourne, Australia, the findings of the Friedman Study, the results produced by such distinguished specialists as Roger Mugford, the British animal behavioural consultant, and Aaron Fletcher of the University of Pennsylvania all tend towards the same conclusion: that owners of pets live longer lives and suffer less from ill-health than those who lack such companionship.

But this chapter concerns Earth's gems, which are matter in its purest form, and which heal by transmitting energies gathered from the rest of the universe to which they are linked by their elements and composition. When we are ill, unhappy, or in whatever way out of sorts, it means that we have allowed ourselves to get off-key with our stars. By their power of transmitting the energies that are vital to us, minerals can restore the balance.

So, as a first step in the process of elementary self-healing, make use of your birthstones, be aware of their powers, fondle them, wear them, place them near you and look at them. At night they can bring healing if placed on a bedside table slightly above the level of the owner's head – under the bed or mattress is not as good.

Next study the descriptions of stones in the following pages which concentrate specifically on their healing properties, and then the list of ailments, both physical and spiritual, and of the stones that can help to cure them. In the process of healing by stones, energy flows from the stone with unstoppable force. But first, it must be warmed to room temperature at least, and possibly rubbed, to activate its vibrations. It is these vibrations that act on the patient to correct his or her own rhythms. It is the stone, moreover, which is doing the work here, simply by virtue of proximity. The patient has merely to let it act.

But beyond this process of simple self-help there is the ancient art of healing others – an art dismissed in the materialistic centuries but now returning, borne along on a steady tide. How can a person tell whether he or she possesses this power? It certainly owes nothing to academic attainment, sharp wits or 'braininess'. It is a matter, rather, of concentration and sensitivity. It is these qualities, and these alone, which will unlock a stone's essence, and whether or not one possesses them one must find out for oneself. One must simply remember that since healing by stones can open up the higher channels of the spirit or soul clogged and blocked by the excesses of rational thought, the healer's own mind must be cleared of débris before useful work can begin. Remember too that the lists just mentioned, which of course are intended as much for the use of the healer of others as of the individual applying a healing remedy to himself, are based on general findings only. The practitioner's skill and personal vibrations are also a factor and so the lists should be used as a springboard for free experiment.

It will be noted, too, that a few ancient and powdered recipes are listed. These are included for fun, and for the sake of curiosity, to illustrate some ancient ideas. They are definitely not advocated by the author. The virtue of gemstones lies in their tints, their reflectivity and their energies.

But first, how does the would-be healer start? How is the healing process performed?

The healing is conducted through the medium of a stone, rather in the manner of crystal-gazing. For the novice, the best choice is a piece of Rock Crystal of the quartz variety, one and a half to two inches long, which should be cleansed before use in pure, cool water, preferably mineral water, and allowed to dry in the Sun or at least the air. It should *not* be dried with a towel, as adhering fluff will collect negativity. Nor is salt water, which leaves an unwanted surface film, suitable for this process of cleansing.

To attune your mind to the mineral, play some soft, gentle music. Then place the crystal at eye level beside a lit candle and focus on the flame. This will have the effect of anaesthetizing the optic nerve, thus cutting out distractions, which is what happens in crystal gazing. With half-shut eyes watch the light expand and let the glow illuminate the far edges of the room. Inhale deeply, then exhale slowly, deliberately breathing onto the crystal.

Now transmit yourself in imagination to some particularly well-loved setting and think of yourself lingering there. Almost at once, your own vibratory rate will begin to adjust itself to the crystal's and your higher channels will clear. Then take your crystal to a peaceful, light place, indoors or outdoors, and, without the candle, concentrate on the stone until its body-light expands. Let its energy field fuzz the air around you while you breathe in the crystal's vibrations. Your own will transfer themselves to the crystal as you breathe out.

Carry your crystal with you, constantly fondle it and, when you are alone, at any time of the day or night, imagine your body, your mind and the crystal in perfect harmony. After a bad experience or a disturbing day, clear your stone with mineral water and let it dry as already described. If need be, light the candle and start the process again from scratch. You will find your crystal will bring peace, acting on your mind like a memory chip in a computer.

From then on, for those who find themselves gifted with this faculty, the healing of others will be an easy step. Only remember that, although each variety of gemstone has its own individual vibrations, and thus its own potential for energy and power, it cannot transmit and amplify these forces until stimulated either through heat or manipulation.

Amplification of the crystal's energy is the key to healing through this medium, in which a mental image of the patient is evoked, wrapped round with the crystal's light. More often than not, when this is done, the truly affected areas, which may be quite different from those in which the pain occurs, will reveal themselves in patches or bursts of muddy or angry colours, marring the even light that constitutes what is known as the aura. The latter, a sort of rainbow of colours mainly around the head, may be a genuinely multi-coloured phenomenon but usually reveals itself by a predominance of two or three. Distinct, strong tints and clarity are all-important in the healthy aura. If these colours are broken or faded, the practitioner mends them by feeding the energy of another gem with the mind's eye. Stones of the Zircon family, with their fine display of light and colour-range, are generally the best for this purpose, but as Zircons may be expensive or hard to obtain, the solution may well be a visit to one's local museum.

There the tyro healer can study selected minerals – not more than four or five at one sitting – and having visualized them thoroughly, will return home, bring out his Rock Crystal and allow the image of the stone or stones studied in the museum to work through it to the patient. If, however, the gem itself can be acquired, place the Zircon next to the Rock Crystal or in the palm of the hand and concentrate fully on the afflicted aura, to send it healing and strength. Hold the aura as steady as possible in the mind's eye for a few seconds, then bathe it mentally with the light from the Rock Crystal. Finally stabilize the aura in the same mental fashion with Labradorite.

All vegetable and animal matter constantly radiates trillions of fine, hair-like, sky-blue arrows – the physical manifestation and gauge of the life-force – which hug the body and flow freely at an even and constant strength when the subject is well, but when continuance of life is in question or the subject is notably weak, the arrows become erratic or sparse. Working with the same Rock Crystal, clear (white) Topaz or Aquamarine, the healer will attempt to coax the emanations back into their proper form. If the subject responds, gently nourish with Rhodonite or Rhodocrosite, in the manner described above. These stones carry the power of unobstructed love. Use Rhodonite for the mature patient, Rhodocrosite for the young. For plants and animals, follow the described procedure with a bath of Dioptase.

Though the techniques described above can be used with the patient present, they are applicable most of all to the branch of the art known as absent healing, when the patient may be anywhere – in another room, another country or another continent, and most probably will not know that healing is taking place. Because of the esoteric quality of such healing, this is in fact the best way. But whether the patient is present or absent, his first need will be for peace. This means that the healer must himself be relaxed and tranquil, able to make full use of his gems with their properties and health-giving powers.

Earlier in this chapter the vibrations of minerals were spoken of. Very few of us, left to ourselves, are sensitive enough to feel them, but here is a method of learning how to do so which requires no more than a little patience.

Begin with a nest of Amethyst crystals. First rub your palms together, then place your outstretched hands just above the stones. Hold them there for a few seconds. If you don't feel a sensation of buoyant coolness try again, and you soon will. This exercise was demonstrated to many 'doubting Thomases' in the rock department of Harrods store in Knightsbridge, London. Their changes of expression from disbelief to the wonder and joy of achievement were memorable to behold.

Energy through Colour

Finally, three other factors in healing by stones deserve special consideration. The first is colour and its importance as a source of power. It is no doubt stating the obvious to say that colour is one of the great pleasures of life. It dazzles us in the paintings of a Gainsborough or a Van Gogh. We respond with emotion to the spectacle of a beautiful sunset. These things bring excitement to our senses and refreshment to our souls. Have we ever realized that they also restore our bodies?

The nine 'chakras' listed below are the principal energy centres in the body and they work through colour. Each one responds to a particular set of colour vibrations which it transmits to the area of the body beneath its control, either directly or through other, minor energy points. In this way they perform their principal role which is to procure for each one of us physical, psychological and spiritual help.

Each energy point can operate more effectively if matched with an appropriate stone. It will also do best on the day of the week traditionally associated with its dominant colour, also authenticated by ancient esoteric lore.

The chart below shows these correspondences at a glance. On the appropriate day in each week focus the mind on the appropriate colour and stone (where there is more than one stone, exercise your preference), concentrating your thought on the area of the body controlled by the energy point for approximately five minutes. If you feel your body particularly drained, this exercise can be conducted more often than once a week – that is, on days not primarily linked with the energy point in question. Here, as in all other aspects of holistic practice, success will come through experience.

Care and Cleaning

Like all other precious and beautiful objects – not to mention people – stones deserve to be treated with loving care. Recall first their origins in the dark bowels of the earth, and their subsequent sojourn, often lasting many centuries, nearer the surface but in regions often cold and damp. Therefore, handle them as this background suggests. Keep them in a dust-proof case and, except for the rarest intervals, protected from all strong light. What are spoken of here particularly are minerals in their natural state. Gemstones which have been cut and polished are obviously toughened up for handling and display. They too are delicate, as will be shown in a moment. But uncut stones remain as vulnerable and sensitive as at the moment when they were retrieved from the earth. Treat them with no less gentleness and respect than you would a fine and aged sheet of rice-paper!

Now to cleaning itself. If a stone is very dirty, with for instance mud or hard soil to be removed (a state an uncut stone may very well be in when you first acquire it), begin by soaking it in cold water to soften the dirt, which can then be removed with the aid of a 'shaggy dog' tooth-brush. Be careful never to chip, scrape or pick at the stone, which could easily suffer damage.

The Nine Major Energy Centres in the Human Body
(Chakras)

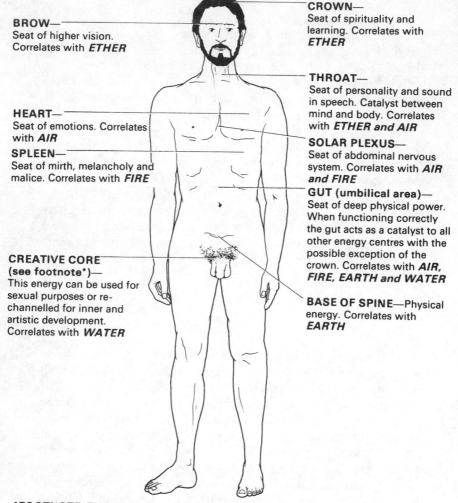

CROWN—
Seat of spirituality and learning. Correlates with *ETHER*

BROW—
Seat of higher vision. Correlates with *ETHER*

THROAT—
Seat of personality and sound in speech. Catalyst between mind and body. Correlates with *ETHER and AIR*

HEART—
Seat of emotions. Correlates with *AIR*

SPLEEN—
Seat of mirth, melancholy and malice. Correlates with *FIRE*

SOLAR PLEXUS—
Seat of abdominal nervous system. Correlates with *AIR and FIRE*

GUT (umbilical area)—
Seat of deep physical power. When functioning correctly the gut acts as a catalyst to all other energy centres with the possible exception of the crown. Correlates with *AIR, FIRE, EARTH and WATER*

CREATIVE CORE (see footnote*)—
This energy can be used for sexual purposes or re-channelled for inner and artistic development. Correlates with *WATER*

BASE OF SPINE—Physical energy. Correlates with *EARTH*

*FOOTNOTE: THE CREATIVE CORE is positioned below the base of the spine on a male. It is above the base of the spine on a female.

Energy Point	Colour	Day	Mineral
Heart	Rich green	Monday	Dioptase, Malachite
Creative Core	Red	Tuesday	Reddish Amber
Base of Spine	Red	Tuesday	Fire Opal, Red Spinel
Crown	Pink-Violet	Wednesday	Pink Sapphire, Kunzite
Throat	Blue-Green	Thursday	Chrysoprase, Turquoise
Solar Plexus	Yellow	Friday	Yellow Citrine, Heliodore
Brow	Indigo	Saturday	Lapis Lazuli, Azurite, Iolite
Spleen	Orange	Sunday	Orange Zircon, Padparadjah
Gut (umbilical area)	White/Pale Blue	Daily	White Topaz, Aquamarine

If, instead of dirt, there are foreign minerals adhering, take the stone to a museum or lapidary shop and ask an expert to remove them.

The cleaning of stones is more complex than might be thought, and it is surprising that few books dealing with minerals bother to mention it. For instance, it is wrong to suppose, though very natural to do so, that all minerals and crystal nests can be washed under running water. On the contrary, this can cause some to disintegrate. Members of the gypsum family (for example, the Desert Rose) take particularly unkindly to water. This is hardly surprising since they are among the main constituents of plaster of Paris, fertilizers, and cement. The same applies to Calcite, the basic compound of chalk and limestone. Other minerals on the danger list include Apophyllite, Sulphur, Halite, Natrolite, Adamite and Auriochalcite, together with all powdery crystals such as often occur in Azurite, Chalcopyrite, Bornite and Citrine, the last-mentioned being, almost invariably, Amethyst reheated by man. If these minerals are dusty, it is best to blow on them, stand them close to an electric fan, or place them in a safe spot which is also exposed to the wind. Alternatively, brush them with a small paintbrush of the finest quality or with a camera lens brush with a puffer bulb.

The majority of large crystals such as Tourmaline, Aquamarine, Rock Crystal and other quartz varieties can be cleaned under cool, running water, rinsed by rainfall, or even washed in luke-warm water containing a tiny drop of detergent and water softener. Be sure to rinse afterwards as the film from the chemicals will not only detract from the lustre of the stone but also attract negativity. After bathing let the stone dry in a shady spot in the open air, or inside on a clean sheet of paper. A towel leaves unwanted fibre particles. And with some stones – particularly Malachite, Azurite, Chrysocolla and Fluorite avoid detergents altogether.

Turning now to gems of the cut and ornamental variety, here is some guidance on the treatment of particular stones.

Solid Opal, when not in use, and particularly if stored in an air-conditioned room, a bank vault, or a velvet-lined box, should be placed in an unsealed plastic bag with a drop of water. A solid Opal should be immersed in cold water about once a month, and should *never* be worn while sun-bathing, swimming, washing up or cooking. If this has inadvertently happened, replenish its thirsty structure with an immediate drink.

Opal doublets and triplets must be left severely alone, for if touched by even a drop of water, or accidentally exposed to heat, they may turn white, lift from their backing, or separate from their crystal dome.

Amber and Jet both take a high polish, are easily scratched, matt on contact with body acids and perfumes, and have low melting points. On account of their fragile characters both will disintegrate and eventually crack on exposure to air. To halt this process, even if they are not being worn, polish them regularly with a soft cloth impregnated with beeswax or with a beeswax furniture polish. Do not let other jewellery touch them – their softness will cause them to rub. Store them in darkness and wrapped in a soft cloth. When fashioned as beads, thread them on silk or cotton – metal will certainly damage them beyond repair.

Turquoise can be rubbed with a soft cloth but must be kept away from heat or it will fuse. Swift discolouration occurs through contact with body oil and cream. Body acids cause discolouration too, so wear Turquoise on the outside of a garment.

Fluorite and Dioptase jewellery must be protected with high settings.

Hematite, sadly, will lose its sheen after about six months' solid wear; there is nothing to be done about this. *Jade* and *Jadeite* are tough, but break if knocked.

Pearls are a difficult gemstone to advise on, as there are so many grades. Generally a light shampoo will not hurt them, but they should not be subjected to ready-made jewellery dips, lemon juice or any acid.

Mother of Pearl and Coral should be cleaned in the same way as pearls, shells, ivory, and all seed jewellery.

Diamonds can be soaked in jewellery dips and cleaned with a 'shaggy dog' brush and a little shampoo. Some people add a dash of ammonia, but that is not to be recommended. Jewellers often clean Diamonds by ultrasonic water heating (that is, heating through the operation of high frequency soundwaves). This is a dangerous practice, as the smallest flaw in a crystal can lead to a split stone. For the same reason *Emeralds*, which have natural striations of colour in the very best, and countless flaws and inclusions in most, can be destroyed by this method. Instead, clean Emeralds with luke-warm water laced with a sniff of shampoo, and rinse afterwards.

Rubies, Sapphires, Topaz, Spinels and Zircons are other precious stones which should not be tortured by ultrasonic as they often lose colour. A good soak in shampoo and water softener is a much better idea.

That famous rock, *Lapis Lazuli*, seems to stay clean all by itself, but if thoughtlessly handled will need a professional polish every now and then.

The care and cleaning of minerals and crystals is an enormous subject, which a lifetime's study would hardly be sufficient to master, but the key to it all is tenderness and respect. No owner or wearer, even the veriest novice, who cultivates that spirit is likely to go far wrong.

Esoteric Cleansing

This can be considered as complementary to practical care, and many weird and wonderful rituals have become attached to it over the centuries. Here is one authentic method.

Sit cross-legged with the back of the hands resting on the thighs in the pyramid position and your stone placed at forehead level. In imagination surround the stone with light and transport it to the edge of a sandy shore to be lapped by the incoming tide. This vision need only be held for a few minutes, as the ocean is a natural disinfectant, and powerfully remedial. Your stone is now regaining harmony from the silicon-rich sand, silicon being the most prolific element on earth and the one all minerals and crystals are attuned to.

Still in imagination, take your stone to a mountain stream

and dunk it. Finally, dry it by a fire spiced with frankincense – an aromatic resin obtained from African and Asian trees.

After this imaginary, meditative operation, physically rinse your stone in mineral water – the bottled kind will do – and let it dry naturally in a shady spot. Cleansed, as it should now be, both physically and spiritually, it is a perfect medium for the esoteric healing act.

A Technique for Meditation

The wartime Resistance heroine Odette Hallowes, awarded the MBE in 1945, The George Cross in 1946, and the Légion d'Honneur in 1950, found relief from excruciating pain at the hands of her tormentors by means of a technique little considered today by the majority of people of a practical turn of mind: the technique of meditation. Her salvation was to concentrate on the ever-changing coloured light thrown off by an opal ring which had – by luck or perhaps by providence – been left on her finger, thus utilizing a means of mental escape from unbearable physical suffering similar to that which other torture victims have been known to employ. Is it coincidental that the Opal in ancient times was reputed to be 'The Stone of Justice' and 'The Rainbow Bridge between Heaven and Earth'?

Meditation, that key to transcendence of worldly cares, can avail itself of many aids, including crystals and stones. Here is a lovely technique which a friend of mine learned from a female Shaman of a North American tribe.

To practise it you will need a blanket, a largish feather (my friend used a brightly-coloured macaw feather), four incense sticks, a Rock Crystal measuring at least four inches in length, a smaller crystal or ornamental stone of whatever sort you care to choose, and a quiet, semi-darkened space in which to work.

To begin, having decided on your meditational theme, lodge it firmly in your mind and write it on four separate pieces of paper. Place these individually with the four lit incense sticks in north, south, east and west positions round you. Spread the blanket on the floor and briskly flick the feather around as a means of banishing any patches of negativity. If at this stage you find the scent of the incense too heady, it may be extinguished.

Seated cross-legged on the blanket, rest the backs of your

hands on your legs, cradle the large crystal in your right palm and the smaller stone in your left. This attitude is known as the 'power-house' position, and forms a triangle, echoing the shape of the pyramids. Now breathe regularly and deeply, completely exhaling your breath each time. Close, or half-close, your eyes, and imagine your body in its present pose surrounded by light. Coax the light until its fullness touches the paper placed near the incense. See the subject from all angles, let it fill your being, understand why it is there, what you must do about it, and who you should pass it onto – if anyone. Sometimes, when subjected to this close and unblinking scrutiny, the subject is seen to lack merit. In that case, discard it.

Should placing the subject on paper, or fixing it in your mind, prove too difficult a task, try an alternative method. After you have positioned your body in the power-house pose and surrounded yourself with light, imagine a wheel containing seven segments of colour. These are the colours of the rainbow – red, orange, yellow, green, blue, indigo and violet. Whirl the wheel. When the motion stops, you will see your subject in one of the segments. Then, as in the first exercise, dwell upon it, observe it with great care, and, if appropriate, apply to it the powers of healing. And, as before, think of how to transfer it for the benefit of others.

When the time has arrived to conclude the meditation, never cut it off suddenly, for as the mind has been working the physical senses have been put to sleep. Wake them gently while still holding the power-house pose. Fade out the image until you see only colour or light. Once again breathe deeply and return the body to life by wriggling your toes, fingers, head, limbs and trunk. Ease yourself to your feet and sign off with a long, cool drink of water, preferably energized by the presence in the glass of Fluorite, a stone which brings oxygen to the bloodstream.

As a luxurious extra, and if you have the time and inclination, lie flat on the floor covered by your meditational blanket and allow yourself to fall asleep. On waking you will feel strong, relaxed and happy. Often you will find that problems you had not even meditated about will have been solved too!

Meditation can be practised during the daytime or at night, each with a different purpose. Night meditation is generally practised with the aim of opening the higher channels of the mind, whereas day meditation is for physical energy, nourishment of the body and spirit, and healing. The best of both worlds can be obtained, in a manner of speaking, by meditation at sunrise. No need to stay up alone to indulge in this. Better still is to do it with friends. Before you launch into this euphoric adventure, take a glass of water which has stood in the night air. If you fancy an elixir let Aquamarine, the life-force stone, be placed in the glass. Choose as your vantage-point a hill, a cliff, or some other spot with a view of the eastern horizon, and find a place where you will be comfortable. Bare your feet and your head and arrange your crystals beside you. Position your body in the pyramid-shaped power-house attitude and be absolutely sure that your palms are exposed to the first streamers of light which herald the Sun and illuminate the sky. You will benefit from the positive ions showered on Earth – magnesium, aluminium, iron and zinc, among others.

From here on all is easy as you are on automatic pilot. Go ahead and enjoy the atmospheric effects of sunrise. Meditate and know that this is an opportune moment for administering healing to others.

Twilight meditation can be equally therapeutic, especially after watching a sunset. The only preparation I personally make for this exercise is to wear a cotton headband containing a Rock Crystal and a sliver of Azurite. One could equally well wear a crystal pendant or necklace and carry the Azurite. Together these minerals assemble suitable ions for this period between night and day when the Sun's centre is below the horizon and the passive side of nature prepares to dominate the active.

Before meditating, there are basic rules that should be followed. Because of negative vibrations picked up from oneself and others, it is wise to start with a bath, and since during meditation body temperature sometimes drops a little, make sure to be warm and comfortable. Never attempt meditation on a full stomach or after consuming alcohol, and certainly not in a crowded room or within earshot of an argument or a party.

Beyond that, there are no rules. Meditation is always therapeutic, with or without stones. Moses used it on the mountain, before receiving the Ten Commandments, and the greatest sages have resorted to it. One thing is certain: the would-be healer with stones will do no good without a spirit of calmness and recollection, which is what meditation, when properly practised, ensures.

Precious Stones, Precious Health: The Healing Stones

Alexandrite

Here is a stone of stunning optical properties. By day, its colour is an intense grass-green. By artificial light it undergoes a trans-formation into a soft columbine-red or a gentle raspberry-pink. Since green is the colour of new growth and pink the shade of impartial love, the Russian name for Alexandrite, 'Stone of Good Omen', could not be more apt.

The Alexandrite has a positive electrical charge which stays for hours after rubbing, and an energy factor which changes with its colour. But potent though this stone looks, it radiates sensitivity. In physical healing it bypasses the actual ailment and goes straight to the root of the problem, acting on the head and spine areas, effectively rebalancing the dry, the moist, the hot and the cold in their correct proportions. Worn by day and night, its beneficial properties soon show. The head feels roomier, the memory improves, eyesight is clearer and the neck muscles are relieved of tension.

The Alexandrite is expensive because rare. A variety of chrysoberyl, it was discovered as recently as 1831, so compared to most gems its history is short. Though tests to establish its efficacy in natural medicine will certainly continue, it has already proved its worth. It transmits inner peace by developing mag-nanimity of heart and should be valued and used extensively.

Amber

This time-hardened resin is associated with healing powers galore, and rightly so. Retsina, the pine-cured, resinated Greek wine, soothes irritated throats as well as raising depressed spirits, while nature's way with wounded vegetation is to heal a plant's cuts with its own secretion of gum. Ancient ointments consisting of powdered Amber mixed with various combinations of oil were similarly applied to human wounds, but this stone's real power lies in the curing of chest complaints such as asthma, bronchitis, coughs, raw throats, headaches caused through chest and throat inflammation, and toothache.

Certain modern healers are reverting to the old custom of mixing powdered Amber with honey as an internal medicament. Beware of this! It is often no more than a money-making racket and can be dangerous to those who take it. Certainly swallow no such mixture except on the advice of an orthodox medical practitioner. Amber heals perfectly well from the outside and this is how it should be used.

For healing purposes, wear it between the levels of chest and ears or, if you prefer to carry it – that is, to use it as a touchstone – place it in a top pocket or in a silk sack on a loose string round the neck. Do not cover the throat chakra – Amber has the wrong vibrations for this area. Similarly do not wear a large piece of Amber for too long a period. Amber is inclined to keep the wearer's energy circulating inwardly instead of allowing it to flow out, thus stunting its owner's physical strength.

Properly used, it brings benefits on every level. For meditational purposes use only the clear fluorescent type found in the Dominican Republic and Sicily. Opaque varieties are gentler in character and promote understanding towards others, probably because they contain trillions of sub-microscopic air bubbles and possibly droplets of water and/or calcite. Many actors and actresses wear Amber and Amethyst in combination jewellery on stage. They are convinced these stones help their performances.

Pressed Amber, which is a mass of small pieces welded together under gentle heat, has almost the same essence as the natural form. The same is generally true of what are known as 'inclusion' pieces – that is, Amber inset with small insects, bird feathers, pine needles, flowers and anything else the once sticky substance embalmed. However, not long ago, a specimen entombing a large lizard was found. When tested for healing purposes it emitted a hefty, negative energy!

Amethyst

This stone, always esteemed, should be accounted especially precious in the hectic world of today, for it heals during sleep, induces meditation, and is thus invaluable for healing and comforting those suffering from stress or from psychosomatic illness. Even cancer, as many researchers now recognize, can be precipitated by mental strain, and the Amethyst, coloured red by irradiated iron, contains the very element with which orthodox practitioners fight the disease. Iron is one of the six active body minerals essential for life. It strengthens the muscles, enriches the blood and increases resistance to infection, so here too the Amethyst has an invaluable part to play.

It is the stone of piety and keeps its wearers from falling into the sin of drunkenness. Bishops' rings are traditionally mounted with Amethyst and that holy monarch, Edward the Confessor, had an Amethyst ringstone. Still in the royal collection, it was once renowned as a charm against contagious diseases.

There was an ancient belief that the Amethyst changed colour when placed near poisoned food. This almost certainly stemmed from the fact that it shows colour variations in its single crystals. It is attuned to the higher sensitivity of the crown energy point which inspires second sight.

Used in combination with a Bloodstone, the Amethyst can be strapped over the area of a blood clot and after a fortnight or so the obstruction often clears. Sometimes the cure is permanent, sometimes the patient will need to repeat the treatment periodically.

Worn with Carnelian, it restrains the overactive and also the bossy – at home, at work or in public life. Did we begin by saying that this was truly a stone for today!

Aquamarine

Every energy has its colour and the energy of our body's life-force is sky-blue. This is the colour of the Earth as seen from space and the tint reflected in the blue of the Aquamarine.

When assessing a person's health many crystal practitioners work through an Aquamarine to gaze at the surrounding life-force, which manifests itself to those sensitive enough to see them in trillions of fine, hair-like blue arrows. If this radiating energy is steady and of constant strength throughout its flow (that is, not patchy), then all is well. If however it is seen to thin out here and there, the indications are that physical strength is on the wane. In this case healing should be applied to the inner centres through the throat chakra, using the Aquamarine as a stabilizer. When the blue arrows strengthen, the patient begins to recover. If the life-force insists on leaving the body, which means that the person is dying, the Aquamarine can hold it for a little time until the departing person is prepared. But the healer must act with care. If the life-force is held in for too long, the dying person will suffer.

Aquamarine once bore the title 'All Life'. The Romans valued its natural six-sided form, so wore Aquamarine earrings, a favoured decoration, with their crystals uncut, not understanding that a stone can be cut or even powdered and still retain its original properties, the stone's internal 'building blocks' of atoms and molecules being as much present then as before. Aquamarine is a gem that must be listened to, not 'ordered about'. Its powers will depend on its owner's receptiveness and it will work on the level that he or she is able to attain.

Apart from the virtues attributed to it in the past, modern practitioners find this blue wonder-stone improves eyesight, calms eye-itch, is an effective balm for swollen feet and a fine soother of jangled emotions and nerves. Its essence being liquid, it refines the faculties of the intuitive mind and removes discordant vibrations.

Aventurine

With its soft energy and slightly iridescent, metallic beauty, this stone was put to beautiful use by the Russian craftsman and designer Carl Fabergé (1846–1920) and also by the Chinese. Its less practical applications, like those of the Carnelian, have, however, lately been overlooked.

Aventurine can be brownish in colour, when it belongs with the feldspar family and is called the Sunstone; or yellow-brown or greenish-yellow, in which case it is known as Aventurine quartz. Both varieties act as a general tonic on the physical level, with special application to the central nervous system.

On a higher level this is a stone for meditation, and for encouraging malleability of mind.

Azurite

Azurite can open the floodgates of cosmic truth and reveal to its wearers the essential purposes of their life. As such, it is a stone for highly evolved souls. People find it an aid to their psychic development but will also discover that its effects last a limited time. For slowly but inexorably this royal to midnight blue stone changes into another mineral, the bright green Malachite.

During its working life as an Azurite, however, it frees channels along which its wearers might fear to tread. In particular it can complete the opening of the 'third eye', the faculty which enables its owner to see and feel the approach of good and evil happenings. In the same way it can be used to transfer the energy of positive and negative vibrations from its manipulator to another person.

Little is known of the Azurite's powers on the level of physical healing, but its hallmark is harmony and encouragement of the qualities of sympathy and tenderness in all their forms. Thus it can assist the physical healer when his patient's ailment is caused through disappointment, aggression or hate.

As Malachite, this stone helps those with bone calcification. But as Azurite it seems to operate almost entirely on the spiritual level alone.

Bloodstone

Holding mightier than Mars energy but still relating to that planet, the Bloodstone, with its traces of Plutonian influence, can weigh too heavily on the mind. For that reason, in healing it should always be used in combination with Rock Crystal and Rose quartz, which will alleviate its oppressive effects.

Containing iron impurities, this stone works with the bloodstream against cramp and light-headedness. Its corrective properties also enable it to break down deep-rooted diseases and counteract over-indulgence, aggression, obsession and violence.

More cheerfully, in its lighter aspects, the Bloodstone encourages a sunny disposition as it sweeps dross from the chakras.

Blue John

There is a strange belief, many centuries old, that the spirits of certain children unhappily aborted, often in the ordinary way of nature, roam about the world in desperation and confusion seeking an earth mother from whom they can take nourishment. The mother, when found, mysteriously loses strength and in recent years some astonishing esoteric cures have been accomplished through the medium of the banded fluorite known as Blue John with which crystal practitioners have treated the 'mother's' blood before it reaches the spirit child. Once this is done the child is 'born' and both woman and infant can be freed by an esoteric severing of the spiritual natal cord.

There is a scientific reason for the efficacy of the stone in that fluoride in the laboratory can be heated with acid to give off bubbles of acid gas. The stone can be similarly stimulated by the crystal practitioner. But while the Blue John is doing its work, other stones will be needed as well: Aquamarine for life-force; Magnetite for polarization (that is, for aligning the spine to the magnetic forces of Earth); and Dioptase to strengthen the heart. These are for the 'mother'. The child spirit, now released, must also be treated as the practitioner thinks fit. No other fluorite works with such success as Blue John in restoring women from the effects of mysterious weakness. Doubtless this is because of the Blue John's concentric purple-blue banding, which is now thought to be caused by radiation from uranium.

Blue John also brings relief to mediums and other sensitives who are overworked and giving too much of themselves. If you live in the country, or any unpolluted area, a chunk or small nodule of Blue John in a bowl of tapwater can also be left outside the house, in the fresh, cleansing air, overnight. It provides an excellent pick-me-up.

Bowenite

Often called 'The Gentle New Jade' or 'Korean Jade', this stone is an unusual, transparent-to-translucent, hard variety of serpentine. It is usually tinted pale sea-green touched with yellow, though the New Zealand variety is a magnificent deep greenish-blue. But whatever its colour this stone is invaluable because of its content of magnesium. It is established that the human body should contain twenty-one grammes of this mineral. If its magnesium count falls below that figure, depression and insomnia set in and Bowenite helps to cure both. It also relieves indigestion and acts as a general antiseptic.

By itself an important throat chakra stone, when worn with Chrysoprase Bowenite has the additional virtue of enhancing spiritual vision and sharpening the wearer's perceptions.

Carnelian (Cornelian)

Once a stone in King Solomon's breast-plate, this now unjustly overlooked gem clears the mind for deep concentration and, when coupled with Amethyst, purifies the consciousness, reverses negative attitudes and develops higher mental awareness. In meditation it induces a better understanding of the true meaning of life and thus offers a key to wisdom.

As both the Carnelian and the Amethyst have iron as a colouring agent, they can be used in combination to benefit the blood stream, combat depression and help their owners to shake off sluggishness and become vigorous and alert.

Chalcopyrite and Bornite

These stones go together like the proverbial horse and carriage. Chalcopyrite is linked with Jupiter, Bornite with Venus. Employed in combination they can help to terminate one of the most agonizing and frustrating states of mind, that of chronic indecisiveness. Beware, however, never to use them to tamper irresponsibly with other people's lives. Both Jupiter and Venus are justice-loving planets, and fiery with it. Any spiteful hanky-panky could rebound on your own head!

Chalcopyrite and Bornite are used by mediums in contacting the deceased. But here they are effective on two conditions only. First the departed must be recently dead and have been personally close to the medium; secondly the deceased should have left unfinished some action of which the completion is truly urgent.

It is important to recall that Chalcopyrite and Bornite are major ores of copper, a mineral vital to our bodies as an activating element to enable the amino acid Tyrosine to work on the pigmentation of the hair and skin. Copper also helps to convert the body's iron into the oxygen-carrying pigment contained in the red blood cells. As Chalcopyrite and Bornite are not only rich in copper but also comprise a fair amount of iron, sufferers from anaemia and edema, two diseases caused by copper and iron deficiency, obviously benefit from their actions.

It is a household truism that if food is cooked or heated in copper pans, Vitamin E, Folic Acid and Vitamin C are destroyed, so strong is the mineral's action. Copper also remains in the body of a dead person long after the other minerals have disappeared, as witness the hair still found to be in good condition when caskets containing the bodies of men and women from the Tudor period were opened recently.

Both Chalcopyrite and Bornite can act with great benefit on the general running of daily life. But so powerful are their energies that after a certain amount of use they will shatter into small pieces.

Chrysocolla and The Eilat Stone

Here are two minerals not often used in physical healing but shown by recent tests to be powerfully efficacious against weakness of the bones and lack of pigmentation in hair or skin. These minerals, both copper based, likewise help the absorption of Vitamin C into the body and assist iron assimilation.

On the spiritual plane, both Chrysocolla and the Eilat Stone can ward off attacks from lower entities such as poltergeists. They are efficient ESP (extrasensory perception) agents which work by opening the throat energy point.

Ideally, tradition holds, both these closely related stones should first come into one's possession as a gift.

Chrysoprase

Here is one of nature's most contradictory stones. The colouring of the Chrysoprase, which runs from translucent emerald through apple-green to yellow-green, is due to the presence of nickel, a metallic element which contributes to many allergies. Yet Chrysoprase purges its wearers both physically and spiritually, from the lowest plane upwards. It is a case of a little poison acting as a vaccine, as with the Diamond.

Both on account of its outgoing influence, which promotes inner clarity and discipline, and of its tint, this protective and strikingly beautiful mineral is often likened to the Jadeite of Upper Burma, though Chrysoprase is the more adept of the two in deflecting negative vibrations before they reach the higher senses. As jewellery or a touchstone, this mineral corrects nervous disorders, steadies the brain before bursts of activity, calms sufferers from convulsions and hysteria and eliminates anxiety. Its 'watchdog' personality protects its owners from over-violent reactions and filters discordant facts until a balance is obtained.

The nickel-tinted variety of this gem, the most sought after, comes from Australia. But here, as always, personal choice is important, and some may prefer the paler types which occur in the USA, the Urals and Brazil. A chromium chalcedony called Mtorodite, from Zimbabwe, is also on the market. In all respects except the colouring agent this stone resembles Chrysoprase, but unlike the latter it has yet to show holistic results.

One curious characteristic of the Chrysoprase is its fidelity to its owner. On changing hands, or when an owner has died, it may show no response at all in the possession of a stranger, which is doubtless why this most personal of gems used to be buried with the deceased in Iron-Age Japanese graves.

Citrine

Natural Citrine was originally an Amethyst transformed by being reheated and burnt in Earth's crust. Then man took a hand, learning to 'cook' this stone artificially. But whether in its natural or man-made form, the energy of this rare and highly desirable gem is so similar as to make no difference.

Citrine is of various colours. The very orange shade helps the spleen; yellow Citrine acts on the solar plexus; the orange-brown, 'madeira' variety is used in Crystal healing, where it relieves the sufferings of introverted personalities by encouraging rational and positive thought. Combined with Amethyst, it purifies the blood and clears the mind. Often it is even more helpful than Amethyst as a means to meditation. This is understandable since the violet of Amethyst and the gold of Citrine are both head colours.

Coral

Filled with negative vibrations, a legacy of the Coral hunters, this ocean gemstone nevertheless does its best, and its healing properties, mainly efficacious against calcified joints and skin eruptions, have been recognized since ancient times.

Coral's astrological correspondence is with the Moon, as befits its watery genesis, and in a chart with a positive placement can have a beneficial influence on anyone born under the same ruling mass. When negatively aspected, however, it can produce arguments and depression. It will often balance a chart with an abundance of fire.

Those who find Coral an attractive stone to wear should follow tradition and respect its natural form. This means wearing it as pieces of twig or cut stems, never fashioned into beads.

Agatized Coral is a strikingly different gem, in which the original calcite has been replaced by fine-grained Quartz in the course of geological changes, yet the essentially protective character of Coral remains. Agatized Coral calms the nerves, aids the digestive system and creates physical harmony of a gentle but pervasive kind.

Diamond

The purest substance in nature and one of the hardest (ten out of ten on the Mohs Scale), the Diamond can be fashioned into the neatest and sharpest of cutting edges and as such has helped to bring into existence one of the marvels of modern medicine, the art of micro-surgery.

Using a Diamond blade instead of the old-fashioned stainless steel is, for a surgeon, the equivalent of switching from manual to power-assisted steering in a car. It requires virtually no pressure so there is minimal scar tissue after the wound is healed, while the blade's smooth cutting track minimizes bleeding. Bruising and after-pain are alike greatly reduced. Blue and Yellow Diamonds of the highest quality are both used. Best of all, however, are the first grade, clear white stones. With the addition of a fibre-optic light attached to the blade's feather-weight titanium handle, the surgeon gets a clear view both of and through the blade which is invaluable in deep cavity operations.

Cost unfortunately prevents these miracle blades from being adopted for general use; and cost, too, disqualifies the Diamond as an instrument of holistic healing, since few can afford the two carat stone which is the smallest needed to produce any results. An uncut Diamond of clear quality could be used, but such stones are hard to obtain, and the quality of light refracted from industrial Diamonds, which are readily available and would be acceptable in terms of price, is so poor as to render them useless.

Tradition endowed the Diamond with a wonderful range of powers, from curing lunacy to driving away the Devil. It was believed to bolster up courage and, above all, to ensure longevity. Thanks to carbon, the single element in its composition, it was also esteemed as a vaccine – a tradition scientifically based. It is unrivalled in its hard surface lustre and dispersion of light (fire). When rubbed, it produces a positive electrical charge.

Last but not least, the Diamond is a token of love. But its coveted reputation as a girl's best friend should not be allowed to rest, as it usually does, entirely on the Diamond's over-bloated market value. Rather this magnificent gem, through its purity and durability, offers moving proof of total perfection expressed in a single element.

Dioptase (The Copper Emerald)

This stone rivals the Emerald (see next entry) in the beauty of its colouring and in its holistic powers. As its nickname indicates, its metallic element is copper, a substance used by nature, in combination with iron, to prevent fatigue and promote resistance to disease. (It also converts iron into the pigment needed by the red blood cells.)

For holistic purposes, Dioptase pendants should be worn mid-chest. Alternatively, a clump of unset Dioptase crystals should be held in the left hand each day for about five minutes, for the third finger of this hand channels directly to the heart, seat of the emotions and all the generous instincts and source, when healthy, of all physical and mental strength.

Nor does Dioptase confine its healing powers only to humans. Sick animals, birds, and plants have been cured by it. Two birds which the author looked after were flooded with Dioptase light, in accordance with the esoteric technique of healing already described, for two minutes a day, then small crystals were placed in the sick bay. Soon both creatures were on the mend. The plants were similarly bathed in the rich, green fire, then soaked in water esoterically infused with Dioptase. The sick animal was a cat, a frightened street dweller with an appalling abcess on its forehead. It would allow no one near, so was mentally surrounded with Dioptase by two devoted pet-lovers at hourly intervals for three weeks. Once again, the treatment worked. Before long, the cat was spotted scampering about, exhibiting a bald patch of perfectly healed skin where an infected hole had once gaped.

Although the brittleness of this stone disqualifies it for cutting, many a magnificent rich-green pendant has been fashioned round a nest of natural Dioptase crystals. Its colour is traditionally linked with non-physical forces and Dioptase itself sharpens the ESP faculties and promotes guidance from higher planes.

Emerald

From the unfathomable depths of this much admired stone come healing vibrations for those afflicted with eye diseases. Testimony to this power has come down to us from ancient times, for in the effigies of gods and goddesses the eyes are often of solid Emerald. Today we can still benefit.

Here are a few hints on how to cure with this stone. When healing your own eyes, simply gaze at the Emerald. If healing those of a patient who is actually present with you, transfer the energy. Alternatively, take a tumbler full of water and soak an Emerald in it overnight. Soak cotton-wool pads in the elixir, wring them partially dry and place them over the closed eyes for about ten minutes twice a day. This treatment is good not merely for diseased eyes. Bloodshot and tired eyes benefit also. If you are unable to get hold of an Emerald, a third method may be used. That is simply to think about an Emerald, transferring the energy to the eye area and the back of the head.

This third method also produces brilliantly beneficial results when applied to the problems of the heart and middle chest. The Emerald is effective too in soothing those with nervous tensions and high blood pressure. On the mental plane it brings tranquillity and balance, hence also learning and wisdom.

Healers may find that it takes some time before they feel thoroughly at ease with this stone, so they should start by working on such comparatively minor complaints as headaches, asthma, the common cold and scalding. Later they will find the Emerald can be used to cure skin ulcers, food poisoning, skin cancer and, many believe, certain other cancers as well.

Ancient crystal practitioners used the Emerald to help relieve the pain of women in childbirth, as an antidote to poison, and for strengthening the memory. Worn by married women, it was thought to guarantee their fidelity to their husbands. Snakes were supposed to be afraid of Emeralds and these gems were also highly regarded as a talisman against evil and the plague. Most important of all was the reputation of the emerald as a link with divine forces.

Fine quality Emeralds are expensive and hard to come by but for healing purposes this does not matter because fortunately for both healers and their patients, a 'mossy Emerald', that is, one which is not quite clear, serves just as well.

Garnet

Black, pink-red, yellow-brown, orange or green – you can take your pick of all these colours when choosing a Garnet, which should properly be regarded less as a single stone than as a member of a vast gemstone family. All Garnets, however, have this in common: they hold a little of most metals but are basically composed of aluminium, silicon and oxygen, and though different stones will be found to suit different patients and healers, holistically speaking all are viable and can be classed as one.

The Garnet's healing character is that of a knight in shining armour. It will send its vibrations straight to the battle front, where other stones have made no impression, and is powerfully effective in lifting depression and strengthening the patient's will to be cured. It is good for treating arthritis and other ailments resulting from calcification. Recently, too, it has been used to help childless couples, aided in this by its high metallic composition and working on the would-be parents both physically and emotionally.

Used in meditation, it brings a sense of relief from material burdens, giving peace and calmness of mind, but working more obviously through the logical rather than the spiritual faculties. When carried in the pocket of an overactive or restless child, or worn as a string of beads, the Garnet will have the effect of channelling the youngster's energy into fewer and less frenetic areas.

Two varieties of Garnet have uses of their own: the orange-coloured stone assists in strengthening the base of the spine, and the green one invigorates the heart.

Heliodore

This lemon to rich-yellow transparent crystal is about to come into its own as an incorruptible medium of spiritual illumination.

Often showing radioactivity and generally thought to be tinted by iron, both of which are emitted by the Sun, the Heliodore indeed resembles a solid chunk of golden light, and in healing radiates a corresponding warmth. It consoles, rejuvenates and achieves its particular power through its ability to reconcile the conscious and the unconscious mind.

Although the Heliodore works through the solar plexus, it actually relates to the circulatory system and heart, where it operates to energize the inner self and the intellect.

(For Hematite see under Magnetite)

Jade and Jadeite

Jade and Jadeite are two entirely distinct minerals with different holistic values, but they are frequently confused and even thought of as one and the same. For that reason it seems sensible to list them together, the better to highlight both their differences and similarities.

Like most gemstones, Jade and Jadeite both contain silicon and oxygen. In addition, however, Jade's composition includes magnesium and calcium, while Jadeite holds sodium and aluminium. Jade is composed of a mass of fibrous, hair-like crystals, while Jadeite crystals are granular.

Containing as it does three of the minerals most needed by the body, that is calcium, iron and magnesium, Jade is a natural medicament for those with high blood pressure, and also for diabetics, those suffering from heart and circulatory problems and people with kidney complaints. It should be worn by pregnant and lactating women, whose condition causes calcium, iron and magnesium to be drained from their bodies at this time.

Jadeite, which in its emerald-green variety adds a touch of chromium to its other mineral constituents, is a muscle strengthener. It also corrects perspiratory problems, counteracts the effects of sun-stroke and, like Jade, is an excellent remedy for high blood pressure.

Both Jade and Jadeite bring peace through serenity and cleanse the energy centres. The green tints of both minerals strengthen the heart chakra while the pink-violet variety of Jadeite induces devotion and favours mystical temperaments.

Jade and Jadeite derive their names from the Spanish word for 'colic', which the Conquistadors called *jada* after the Mexicans had taught them to cure their stomach complaints by touching the affected area with this stone. The geological term for Jade is Nephrite, from the Greek word *nephro* meaning kidney, hence the English 'Nephritis' meaning inflammation of the kidneys. Those acquainted with the legend of the Golden Fleece will remember the Jade axe mentioned in the story which cured kidney complaints. Jadeite means 'like Jade', but the differences should now be clear.

Jasper

This opaque variety of orangey-quartz was famous among the ancients for extracting the poison from snake bites. In early times too it was revered as the supreme rain-bringer and it was also believed that it would lower the blood pressure if engraved with the likeness of a lion.

Today it has largely lost favour as a healing stone. Nevertheless it can help those beset by emotional problems, whether these are caused by feelings of guilt, the loss of loved ones or fear of the future. Its power to strengthen and console such sufferers is well proven.

Jet

This intensely black stone began its existence about one hundred and eighty million years ago when branches and trunks of enormous monkey puzzle trees then flourishing on Earth broke and fell into pools of stagnant water or were carried out to sea by the currents. The waterlogged wood then sank to the waterbed where it was covered with mineral-rich mud and decaying life, which both compressed the embryonic stone and induced chemical changes.

Jet comprises 12 per cent mineral oil. It also shows traces of sulphur, aluminium and silicon, which the skin absorbs when the stone is worn. If friction is applied to the Jet it develops static electricity and, since in reality it is a sort of brown coal, it proceeds to burn, emitting a pungent smell. Sufferers from sinus blockage, the common cold and breathing difficulties are sometimes encouraged to inhale burning essence of Jet. In ancient times the stone was used against toothache, headache, epilepsy, dropsy, loose teeth and swollen feet.

At one time Jet was also invoked as a test for virginity. The stone would be steeped for three days in water or alcohol, removed and given as an elixir to the lady whose virtue was questioned. If the effect was diarrhoea, as well it might have been one may well think, the test was negative. In Spain Jet is still used to ward off the Evil Eye. It is carried in the form of a carving known as a *higa*, which depicts a hand with the Sun pressed between two fingers. Nowadays neglected as a stone to bring good luck, throughout the Bronze Age it was considered one of the most propitious and magical of all amulets and talismans.

Labradorite

When in trouble wear Labradorite. Carry a slice or chunk of this stone in your pocket, place it above the car's dashboard, by the kitchen sink or behind your head whilst sleeping – anywhere you choose, in fact. But be sure to let light catch its iridescent colours which rival a tropical butterfly's wings.

This beautiful extension of a common field rock has an internal structure of repeated layers of microscopically small crystals lying side by side and head to heel. The pale grey, translucent variety of this stone gives better results than the dark, opaque sort. In the former case the light plays more effectively on the stacked crystals which, on account of the optical interference they suffer, produce yellows, pinks, greens, blues and violet-blues, and violet in different shades.

The composition of Labradorite includes tiny plates of iron. These are helpful in straightening the spine and bringing the vertebrae in line with the magnetic north and south poles on Earth, an effect known as polarization. When the stone is used for healing purposes, salt should be taken with food. This gem is now just starting to be recognized. It is the stone of today and of the future.

Lapis Lazuli

This gem contains specks of brassy-yellow or silver-coloured iron, and sometimes of gold too. In fact it is a mixture of at least five separate minerals, which makes it technically a rock and not a stone.

It has a corrective energy directed towards the self which shields the wearer during the process of spiritual development and it allows its wearer to draw wisdom from natural sources. As a result the recipient's emotions are not ignored but appreciated for what they are – an invaluable means of restoring body and mind.

Lapis should be used on the crown chakra or centre forehead, either held in position under a band or worn as earrings or a short necklace. It should not be worn for long periods at a time, not even all day, because such is its strength that it can elevate the higher senses until a receptive owner may want nothing else but its refining energy, leaving no thought for the body which houses the spirit.

Lapis can be a fine transmitter in the hands of a practitioner channelling health to a patient. Most sensitives, however, should cleanse with Lapis rather than use it for the purpose of direct healing until the patient's strength and self-assurance are perceived.

So many healing virtues are attached to this rock that it is difficult to specify the most important. The ailments against which it is particularly efficacious include disorders of the blood, epilepsy, severe stomach pains, vomiting, diarrhoea and brain disease. Lapis is an emotional sanctuary.

Magnetite (Lodestone)

Once known as The Lovers' Charm, this stone is renowned for its magnetic attraction to iron and also for pointing to the north and south poles when hung from a thread. Hence it was thought that it would reconcile quarrelling couples if the wife carried a lodestone and her husband iron shavings. Today its magnetic energies are used for correcting spinal alignment and thus for relieving headaches caused through bad carriage and other discomforts associated with the lack of polarity.

In association with brown or smoky quartz, Magnetite is a suppressive agent for cancerous growths in their early stages. In conjunction with Carnelian, it encourages concentration and promotes wisdom.

There are a number of ailments in the cure of which iron is needed but not the electrical properties of Magnetite and in these

cases the prettier, shiny, steel-grey Hematite can be substituted.
Used in combination with Lapis Lazuli and malachite, or with a
Dioptase pendant, Hematite relieves inflammation of the joints,
increases resistance to disease and prevents fatigue, particularly
during pregnancy. The ancients described Carnelian, Hematite,
Magnetite (Lodestone) and Malachite as antidotes to melancholy. On the basis of modern findings they would seem to have
been correct.

Moonstone

This stone was much used in the past for curing lunacy. However
its lustre, its most important healing quality, acts on its wearer's
negative as well as positive emotions and is therefore a two-
edged weapon when dealing with conditions of the mind. Most
modern practitioners restrict it to the physical side, where it is
particularly helpful in cases of obesity, water retention and
vomiting.

Poor quality Moonstone, which looks almost opaque and is
tinted whitish-grey, is of little help in healing, either to practitioner or owner, but the clearer, blueish variety curbs selfish-
ness and vindictiveness. It also has a generally uplifting effect
when worn by people with a predominant moon in their astrological chart.

In India the Moonstone is a sacred gem and thought to be
lucky if given by a groom to his bride.

Obsidian

When a practitioner finds frustration blocking the healing
process in one of his patients, he turns to Obsidian to counteract
the offence. This is because Obsidian itself is said to hold
negative energies.

In fact Obsidian is not a stone but a form of natural glass,
which has no internal structure but starts in a liquid form. If,
for instance, you look carefully at very old church windows,
you will see the glass in them is thicker at the bottom than at
the top and under magnification the flow lines are obvious.

The healer works on the liquid properties of this natural glass which we call Obsidian. First he transfers the patient's negative energy to the glass, then mentally heats the latter to an elevated temperature. Then comes the moment for a snap deep-freeze which purges the Obsidian and the patient's mind with it. To complete the cure the patient should be immediately bathed in a mental emulation of Rose Quartz, followed by Aquamarine.

Opal

Bringing miraculous order to a wealth of patterns and colours, this, the loveliest variety of our most abundant mineral, quartz, unites heaven and earth in a union of water and fire. It is the stone of hope and justice, the enemy of greed and corruption in all their forms, the support of the righteous – but only the righteous – in war and in the courtroom. Upstart and tyrannical monarchs, exploiting the miseries of their subjects, were once terrified of this gem. Alexander the Great proudly wore an Opal in his girdle but Queen Elizabeth I, though she collected Opals, was frightened to wear one.

The last two Emperors of Russia and their families believed that Opal held the qualities of the 'Evil Eye' and withdrew for the rest of the day after contact with even the smallest of these stones. Queen Victoria amassed more Opals than any other monarch and gave one to each of her daughters on their wedding days but was seldom seen wearing one herself.

The tints of the Opal have been aptly likened to an innocent child's love. The Opal is considered capable of opening the 'third eye' and above other minerals is used by mystics to lead them into supernatural realms.

It is a modern fallacy that Opal is too strong to wear near any part of the body except the extremities. This foolish mis-interpretation of ancient and wise stone lore has been our loss, since Opal protects all the areas of the body that emit heat and all the energy points of attunement – that is, those that receive and dispatch power through colour. The predominant Opal tints to use on these zones are as follows:

Crown: violet and pinkish
Brow: deep blue with yellow, violet and paler blue
Throat: soft greens and pale blue
Heart: the brighter the green the better

Solar Plexus: yellow
Base of Spine: rich red
Spleen: orange purple

In general one should hold the stone near the area concerned for about five minutes daily, depending on one's individual reactions and sensitivity. But provided a clear and strong image of the stone is evoked, healing can occur without the presence of the Opal, on the same principal as absent healing.

In the old days, as a rule, Opal was either burnt or powdered. Today we know that far more effective results are obtained by not tampering with the stone in this way but using it in all its beautiful entirety to tap nature's vital forces for Opal is not efficacious only in the psychic realm. It is of real aid in making good deficiencies on the physical level and, with zones and colours correctly matched as above, will work wonders in feeding the undernourished parts.

This becomes understandable once it is realized that the basic symptom of all disease is colour acting in the wrong places, vibrating out of tune, and thus causing disharmony.

Opal also acts as a protective substance for certain tiny, oceanic growths known as Diatoms. Life on Earth could not go on without the Sun and water, fire and fluid, yet these pairs of opposites cannot meet without a mortal clash, so Diatoms have developed skeletal Opal structures which shield their softer parts from salt dehydration and the ocean's crushing pressure while allowing warmth and light to nourish them. When these minuscule water-bound entities die, their exquisite shells sink down, adding about three million tons of Opal silica a year to the sedimentary rocks on which they come to rest. Modern industry uses this silica in water-repellent ointments and lubricants, so the Opal has this very practical use in addition to all its others.

It also teaches a lesson. Man cannot live without water and its life-giving and purging powers. Indeed water covers roughly three quarters of the surface of planet Earth and man's own constitution is approximately three-quarters fluid. Opal, in addition to silicon and oxygen, contains more water than any other mineral – up to twenty-two per cent. Thus it mirrors the Sun through water, the key of life, speaking to us in an alphabet of colours we understand.

Pearl

This ocean gem is beautiful as a jewel but of less consequence in healing. From antiquity onwards, Pearls were regarded as symbols of chastity and guardians of maidenhood, but their medical virtues were rated low.

The Pearl grows as a kind of cancer in the body of a marine creature. In its natural state it is conceived by a grain of sand or similar small 'annoyance'. The cultured variety can be seeded (that is, started) by the insertion of a plastic or shell marble into an oyster, mussel, conch or clam. In the cultivation of freshwater and seedless Pearls minute particles of chopped foreign flesh are applied to living sea animals, which coat them with secretion, hoping to lessen their discomfort. A refinement of this method is when such Pearl 'slaves-to-be' are brought to the factory by fishermen, there to undergo the attentions of the female staff who open their shells, fasten their feet with clamps, then make ten incisions on the mantle of each victim, forcing lumps of another clam into the cut. This 'Frankenstein' operation completed, the afflicted creatures live in plastic buckets three feet below water level for three years. They are then brought to the surface where the seedless Pearls are removed, the foreign substance having disintegrated in the intervening, formative period.

If all this sounds (and is) monstrous, it has to be said that the glorious, unique natural Pearl is not found fully formed on the sea shore, the river bank or ocean bed. Usually this soft natural marvel of luminosity is prised from a living, breathing child of Neptune which then dies in an unsavoury, smelly mass of seething maggots and other sea creatures imprisoned in a pool or similar closed area.

Many healers past and present have considered Pearls to hold negative energies of a kind to foster human greed. In the light of the foregoing description this conclusion is hardly surprising. Yet maybe a flash from an X-ray camera could put paid to any harmful vibrations emanating from this beautiful jewel. Also to be considered are its constituents of calcium and lime. These (like the Dolomite's) could help to produce the 20 per cent bone replacement every adult needs each year and even help women with menstrual cramp problems and calcium deficiencies.

Peridot

Some say the inhabitants of legendary Atlantis gazed into the rich green velvety depths of the Peridot and chose it as their favourite gem. It was prized by the Crusaders, who found in it the virtue of trust, while the Victorians believed it imparted gracious manners and serenity.

Comprising magnesium, iron and silicon, the Peridot fosters cardiovascular health, converts blood sugar to energy and promotes muscle functioning. It also counteracts some of the physical effects of alcohol. But crystal practitioners use it mainly in the cure of ailments of the digestive system, stomach acidity and unwanted calcium deposits.

Its refined and delicate vibrations make it helpful to the timid, while its very gentleness, in notable contrast to the powerful physical force of many other minerals, relates it to the heart and balances the higher mind.

Rhodocrosite (Inca Rose)

Only discovered about fifty years ago, Rhodocrosite, like its cousin Rhodonite, is new in holistic terms. It is found in two varieties: the sunset-coloured stone of gem quality; and the white-lined, rose or baby-pink semi-precious gemstone. Recent tests have shown that both have beneficial properties, emitting light vibrations which cheer the depressed, preserve youth, and retard the process of ageing, and helping to coax back the life-force into young but sickly subjects as described at the start of this section.

Rhodonite

This gem, like its cousin Rhodocrosite, just described, is young and thus relatively untested in healing terms. But this gem-quality crystal, the colour of crushed strawberries, is a stone of the present and future.

It carries a healing energy tuned to the thyroid gland where, thanks to its manganese content, it produces the hormone thyroxin. It also has beneficial effects on the central nervous system, countering irritability, refreshing the bodies of the tired, weak and old (see, again, the start of this section), and aiding digestion and muscles.

The Rhodonite is best worn on the third finger of the left hand, from which position, attuning itself to the heart, it induces compassion, harmony and sensitivity to the higher values.

Rock Crystal

To the Greeks Rock Crystal, otherwise clear quartz, was holy water frozen by the gods on Olympus. To the Japanese it was the solidified breath and saliva of their sacred dragons, traditionally depicted by artists as violet or white. It has sparkled down the centuries from princely diadems and ecclesiastical crowns and glowed more sombrely among the urns and tombs in impressive burial vaults.

Most cut quartz is hewed sphere-shape, and these carefully fashioned 'rounds' were once used to cure livestock, produce better harvests and call down rain or alternatively the warmth of the Sun.

It was, and still is, the stone most favoured for crystal gazing or scrying, for its lustre quickly freezes the optic nerve, with the result that outside impressions are suppressed and the eye is released to gaze at what is within. This, and the energy built into the quartz, accounts for its overall powers of healing. Its vibrations, which begin at about room temperature, resonate with the triple-time, waltz-like beat of life, giving this mineral a co-ordinating role in all holistic practice. Whether held by a person, placed on an animal or positioned in close proximity to vegetation, Rock Crystal enlarges the aura of everything near it. It even increases the healing powers of other minerals.

Healers who operate by touch rather than by working through gems nonetheless often find that they obtain swifter results when the patient holds a clear piece of quartz. This is because the mineral steps up energy and clears chakra blockages. Scrying with quartz also has a healing aspect, since the process of obliterating external distractions facilitates meditation and the development of the higher self, thus opening channels for the transference of energy from practitioner to patient in the course of absent healing. In short this common and inexpensive stone holds a place of unique importance in the universe of gems.

Rose Quartz

Unobtrusive though it is, this stone should never be underrated. The minuscule crystals of which it is composed give it amazing durability, and the addition of titanium, a metallic element of profound strength, not only accounts for its agreeable colouring but gives it the power to work on scar tissues, soothing and softening them and taking away the pain.

Coupled with Hematite, this pale pink gemstone works wonders on aching bones and bruised skin. Directing its energies mainly through the heart and eyes, it calms the spirit and banishes fear. Violent personalities cannot survive in its vicinity.

Ruby

Of the Ruby, Eastern mythology says: 'This gem is a drop of blood from Mother Earth's heart'; and certainly in terms of healing it is diseases of the blood which are the focus of its special powers. Some say Rasputin made use of a Ruby in treating the haemophiliac son of Tsar Nicholas II of Russia. There is also an ancient Burmese belief that a Ruby worn near or inserted into the flesh of a warrior would prevent him bleeding if wounded. Crystal practitioners use Rubies as a cure for anaemia, poor blood circulation and heart disease, and for cleansing the blood. The liver also benefits from the Ruby's purifying action, as does the brain.

In times past the Ruby was considered efficacious against envy, nightmares, loss of or damage to property, and unfaithfulness in a spouse. It was thought to alleviate pain when worn or carried and to pale or turn black through a change in its vibrations if its owner's life came under threat. It will be found that it promotes disinterested love and acts on the level of extra-sensory perception as a perfect channel of loving communication.

Like the Diamond, it also has a vital role in micro-surgery. Though the Diamond is harder and almost unbluntable unless abused, the Ruby is possibly its superior as a cauterizing instrument.

All this, and beauty too!

Sapphire

Related to the Ruby (a fact few people are aware of), this remarkable stone comes in a whole range of colours, each with its healing virtues, associations and range of powers. Best known and best loved is the dark blue variety, the austere beauty of which is reflected in its effects. The least passionate of stones, this dark blue Sapphire acts directly on the intellect, and perhaps for that very reason is often the subconscious choice of those who wish to suppress their emotions and fall back instead on the reassurance of status and wealth. In healing terms it is excellent against fevers, neurosis and illness brought on by afflictions of the nerves, including asthma.

By contrast, the cornflower Sapphire and other vibrant blues are reputed to lengthen life, keep their wearers looking young, fortify the heart, nourish the central nervous system and heal eye infections.

The almost opaque Star Sapphire has a generally calming effect, helpful in curing stomach ulcers and restraining the over-practical.

The pink-violet Sapphire encourages selfless love. If worn with the traditional dark blue Sapphire it will help its owner to a more humane and sympathetic outlook on life, less narrowly legalistic and more open to the natural emotions.

The Padparadjah or orange Sapphire improves the character of the selfish, particularly those of an apparently extrovert nature who in reality seldom think about anybody except themselves. The energy of this variety of Sapphire works effectively through the spleen, curbing the hastiness sparked off by irritability and encouraging its wearers to think before they act.

Sodalite

In colour this stone is very similar to Lapis Lazuli but its effects
are quite different and confusion of the two is unfortunate.
Sodalite's main holistic purpose is to impart youth and freshness
to its wearer and to those who are treated by its vibrations.

Sodalite could be called 'the stone of mental change or trans-
formation', for it brings back joy and relieves the heavy heart.
Placed just above the head during sleep, it can make a sad person
wake up full of effervescence and bounce.

Sick animals and house plants will respond to a Sodalite used
in combination with Dioptase and Rock Crystal. However, do
not try to place a pendant on an animal, a procedure which
could be dangerous and to which it would very properly take
exception. Instead, amass a generous number of the stones and
place them near the pet's favourite spot. In the case of house
plants, soak the minerals in water for twenty-four hours, then
remove them and treat the plant with the elixir thus produced.

Spinel

Up to the end of the Middle Ages, the Spinel was admired for
the magnificent stone it truly is and was credited with the same
healing powers as other valuable gems of like colourings. This
was before the study of precious stones became a science. Sadly
this beautiful crystal then lost its popularity because both in its
appearance and in its elements as then known it too closely
resembled the Ruby and Sapphire.

We now know that first grade Spinel is far rarer than most
of the stones it could be mistaken for. Unfortunately, however,
the trade still retains the outdated mentality of those early
gemmologists, with the result that the public have not been
given the chance to rediscover it for themselves. In fact it is
similar in composition to many Garnets, though far lovelier in
its sparkling clarity and wonderful range of hues.

It is a hardwearing stone – more so indeed than the Garnet,
Zircon, Emerald, Peridot or Jadeite – and occurs in the same
crystal systems as the Diamond.

Magnesium and aluminium make up the pure, clear-white
variety of this stone, other chemicals, most often iron and

chromium, entering in as impurities to account for its coloured forms, with zinc producing the very scarce blue. These colour differences allow the Spinel to be used in holistic work in place of many Garnets, in particular to promote the functions of nerve and muscle, to diminish stress and to fight the effects of stomach acidity and depression.

The planets Venus and Uranus are co-rulers of this stone, with the result that the Spinel, on the spiritual plane, is effectively directed towards promoting general idealism through harmony, creativity and in particular the making of music.

Topaz

An excellent touchstone or pocket companion, white Topaz especially helps those who suffer from nerves or insomnia. Topaz of all colours is used to heal coughs and throat disorders, all nerve ailments, catarrh, children's diseases such as measles, as well as scabby skin punctures and gout. In Roman times Topaz was used to ward off the effects of black magic and, if strapped over a woman's abdomen during her menstrual period, was reputed to alleviate her pain and discomfort.

As a talisman the most important, indeed unique, virtue of this stone was to protect its owner against sudden death. It is also, in common with certain other gems, said to be helpful in putting its owner in touch with life in other parts of the galaxy.

Tourmaline

Here we have a master physician of the mineral world, with remarkable properties and a harlequin personality. Its myriad tints are the result not of impurities, as is usually the case, but of the contributions made by each single original crystal in this lovely stone's composition.

In times past the Tourmaline was classed as a mineral magnet rather than as a gem. The reason for this was its unique electrical energies which cause it, when rubbed or heated, to produce in each of its crystals a positive charge at one end and a negative charge at the other.

In healing its principal function is to produce polarity, an invaluable virtue since a perfectly aligned spine with feet and senses equally firmly planted on the ground makes it possible to give and receive on all levels.

Each Tourmaline crystal contains aluminium, boron, iron, lithium, magnesium, potassium, silicon and sodium, with most gems showing trace elements of other much needed body chemicals. Magnesium is associated with common and epsom salts which cleanse the system; it is the curative essence of ocean water and is necessary for a good memory. Boron has been used down the ages as a treatment for diseased vocal chords, sore throats and throat inflammations. Potash is found in 'miracle waters' and with fluorine, another common mineral, is used in shrinking troublesome varicose veins and in preserving healthy teeth, bones, nails and hair.

Other uses to which Tourmaline can be put are as a cure for indigestion, lethargy, excessive weight gain and loss, gout and the intense pain of neuritis. The last mentioned ailment can be relieved by the action of Tourmaline in feeding the muscles and releasing trapped nerves when the cranium joints are reslotted into their correct position through the force of its magnetism.

Tourmaline acts well in combination with gold. Rather than encasing the gem in this metal, however, it is better to use an open claw setting which allows the electrical properties of this mineral magician to act without obstruction.

Although Tourmaline is principally effective in physical cures, it is also of assistance to the higher mind through its action in clearing the chakras and removing bodily pain. It is a lovely stone and those who possess one, and particularly those who have been given one, are exceptionally fortunate.

Turquoise

The fame of this stone dates back to the earliest times. It is associated with Hator, daughter and wife of the Egyptian Sun-God Ra, who protected her father and husband from all who rebelled against him and was feared as 'the eye of Ra'. Later it was esteemed by the North American Indians, who believed that it contained the essence of the harshness of winter and would thus ensure that its wearer would show severity towards his enemies. The Buddha used Turquoise to call up spiritual help when he wished to free himself from an unknown and particularly frightening entity. Stories about the Turquoise can likewise be found in Persian, Bedouin, Chinese, Mexican, Tibetan and Turkish mythology. The stone has always been worn as a protection against dark forces. Above all it is the talisman most favoured by horse and rider, and by lovers as a guarantee of mutual fidelity.

Aluminium, alongside copper and a small amount of iron, are the elements composing this opaque but attractive mineral. In healing its principal action is on the throat chakra, though it need not be placed directly over that area since it transmits its energy to all the body zones, particularly the higher abdomen. It is used holistically to cure headaches, eye ailments, fevers, leg, foot and loin problems, and counteracts the negativity which, coming at us in heavy doses, can entangle our lives to the point of chaos and insanity.

It can be used effectively in conjunction with Lapis Lazuli to deflect lowering influences and to harmonize the higher self. It can be set with silver, which does not affect its vibrations, and American Indian craftsmen have often mounted it in this way. But it is even stronger when surrounded or engraved with gold and as such is a necessary filter for other influences and a powerful talisman.

Whatever its shade, this ancient jewel will be found effective as long as its owner feels at ease with the colour of his or her choice. Turquoise exercises a particularly definite influence for better or worse according to the circumstances. It is a stone in which one man's meat is another man's poison and all the more fascinating for that.

Zircon

This many-coloured, transparent gem should not be under-estimated either as a jewel or as a means to holistic healing. Thought by the ancient Greeks to strengthen the mind and bring joy to the heart, the Zircon once took precedence over almost all gemstones on account of its lustre and its dazzling reflection of light, in this respect often rivalling the faceted Diamond. Containing the radioactive element of uranium, the rare metal thorium (used in electrical apparatus) and the precious metals zirconium and hafnium, both of which are employed in the nuclear industry, the Zircon holds within itself the essence of the Sun and Jupiter, which carry the energy of existence.

The overriding characteristic of this crystal is its vitality, which acts with the effectiveness of a laser beam to cure brain damage, venereal diseases and acute skin disorders. It also disperses fluid in the lungs and cures inertia and ailments of the spleen. On the spiritual plane it promotes self-development and the extension of the higher mind, an effect particularly noticeable when the heat-treated sky-blue variety is used.

Although similar to the Diamond in its lustre and light, the Zircon is less authoritarian in character but still firm in its direct action on physical and psychological states of being.

Glossary of Stones in Healing

This list of illnesses, symptoms, and physical and spiritual conditions indicates the stones appropriate to the treatment and improvement of each. Detailed descriptions of the principal stones are given in the preceding pages.

SYMPTOM : STATE	STONES
Abdominal Colic	White Coral
Accidents (prevention of)	Yellow Carnelian
Acidity	Green Jasper, Bismuth, Peridot, Dolomite
Ageing (to retard general process of)	Rhodocrosite, Sapphire, Diamond, Sodalite
Aggression (moderation of)	Bloodstone
Alcoholism	Amethyst
Allergies	Zircon
Anaemia	Metallic Sphalerite, Bloodstone, Citrine, Chalcopyrite, Ruby
Anger	Carnelian/Amethyst
Angina	Bornite, Emerald, Dioptase
Animals' Illnesses	Dioptase
Arthritis	Apatite, Malachite, Garnet, Azurite
Asthma	Amber, Rose Quartz
Aura (strengthening of)	Zircon
Aura (protection of)	Diamond
Aura (stabilization of)	Labradorite
Babies (physical development of)	Rhodocrosite, Sodalite, Dioptase, Chrysocolla, Chalcopyrite
Backache	Sapphire, Magnetite, Hematite
Bad Temper	Heliotrope, Emerald
Belching	Beryls
Benevolence (promotion of)	Jade
Bile Ducts	Jasper, Emerald
Biliousness	Emerald
Bites (venomous)	Sulphur, Emerald, Sard
Bladder	Jasper, Jade, Tourmaline

Bleeding	Ruby, Bloodstone
Blood Circulation	Ruby, Bloodstone, Amethyst
Blood Cleanser	Tourmaline, Red Coral, Ruby, Amethyst
Blood Clots	Amethyst, Bloodstone, Hematite
Blood Pressure (high)	Jadeite, Jade, Chrysoprase Emerald
Blood Pressure (low)	Ruby, Tourmaline
Body Fluids (cleansing of)	Halite
Body Repair (promotion of)	Apatite
Boils	Sapphire
Bones (aching in)	Magnetite, Spinel, Rose Quartz
Bones (health of)	Angel Skin and White Coral Calcite
Bowel	Yellow Jasper
Brain	Pyrolusite, Pyrite, Ruby, Green Tourmaline
Brain Damage	Zircon
Brain Tonic	Coral, Lapis Lazuli
Breathlessness	Magnetite, Amber, Jet
Bronchitis	Amber, Jet
Brow Energy Point	Blue Play on Black Opal, Lapis Lazuli, Azurite, Iolite
Bruises	Rose Quartz
Burns	Chrysoprase, Jadeite
Calcification	Garnet, Calcite, Scapolite, Coral, Pearl
Cancer	Amethyst, Brown and Smoky Quartz, Magnetite
Cancerous Growths	Amethyst
Cancer (skin)	Emerald, Amethyst
Catarrh	Topaz
Cauterizing (for use in surgery)	Ruby
Cell Rejuvenation	Rhodonite, Jasper
Cellular Structure	Indigolite
Central Nervous System	Aventurine
Chakra Blocking (removal of)	Azurite, Lapis Lazuli, Bloodstone
Change of Life	Lapis Lazuli, Garnet, Pearl
Chastity (promotion of)	Sapphire
Chest (relief of pains in)	Amber, Emerald, Dioptase
Chicken Pox	Pearl, Topaz
Childbirth (pain during)	Emerald
Childbirth (to encourage)	Verdite, Emerald
Cholera	Malachite
Circulation (improvement of)	Blue John, Ruby

Clarity	Jade
Cold (common)	Emerald, Jet
Coldness	Topaz, Opal
Colic	Malachite, Jade
Colon	Yellow Jasper
Colour (skin tone)	Iron Stones
Concentration	Carnelian
Concern (alleviation of)	Sodalite
Constancy	Opal
Constipation	Ruby
Consumption	Pearl
Convulsions	Diamond, Blue Zircon
Corns	Rub with Apatite soaked in seawater
Corrective Agent (for character improvement)	Lapis Lazuli, Carnelian
Coughs	Amber, Topaz
Courage	Diamond and all orange stones
Cramp	Limestone, Bloodstone
Creativity	Spinel, Smoky Quartz
Crown Energy Point	Pink Sapphire, Siberite, Iolite
Deafness	Tourmaline
Decay (physical)	Pearl, Blue John
Delirium	Chrysolite
Delusions	Carnelian
Depression	Spinel, Dolomite, Rhodocrosite, Bowenite, Lapis Lazuli, Jade, Garnet, Selenite
Despair	Heliodore
Devotion (to increase)	Pink-Violet Jadeite
Diabetes	Diamond
Diarrhoea	Malachite
Digestion	Olivine
Dizziness	White Sapphire
Disease (contagious)	Dioptase
Disease (general)	Dioptase, Amethyst
Dropsy	Diamond, Moonstone, Jet
Drunkenness	Amethyst
Dysentery	Emerald
Ear Trouble	Sapphire, Amber, Tourmaline
Eczema	Sapphire
Edema	Chalcopyrite, Bornite
Endurance	Jade
Energy	Amber, Jasper, Peridot
Envy	Ruby

Epilepsy	Onyx, Jasper, Jet, Tourmaline, Lapis Lazuli
ESP	Dioptase, Garnet, Ruby
Evil Eye	Jet, Turquoise
Eye Ailments (general)	Emerald, Dioptase, Turquoise
Eyes (bloodshot)	Emerald
Eye Itch	Aquamarine
Eyesight	Goshenite, Malachite, Rose Quartz, Aquamarine, Variscite, Emerald
Eyes (watery)	Aquamarine
Fainting	Lapis Lazuli
Faithfulness (encouragement of)	Ruby
Fatigue	Metallic Sphalerite, Staurolite, Dioptase, Hematite
Fear	Rose Quartz, Emerald
Feet (health of)	Aquamarine, Jet
Fertility (to increase)	Verdite, Orange Sapphire (Padparadjah)
Fever	Chrysoprase, Sapphire, Olivine
Fidelity (promotion of)	Turquoise, Pink Diamond
Flatulence	Emerald, Green Garnet
Fluid (excess)	Jade, Diamond, Heliodore
Fluid (lack of)	Moonstone, Scapolite
Food Poisoning	Emerald
Forgetfulness	Tourmaline, Emerald, Moss Agate
Fractures	Magnetitie, Calcite
Frights	Lapis Lazuli, Opal
Frustration	Obsidian
Gall	Hiddenite
Gallstones	Dolomite, Jasper, Coral
Gastric Fever	Jasper, Emerald
Gastric Ulcer	Emerald, Sapphire
General Tonic	Tiger Eye, Amber, Sard, Padparadjah, Aventurine, Blue John
Glands (swollen)	Topaz
Goitre	Amber
Good Wit	Diamond, Operculum
Greed (moderation of)	Opal
Grief	Lapis Lazuli
Growth (promotion of)	Sphalerite, Galena
Gums (health of)	Pyrolusite
Gut (umbilical area)	White Topaz, Aquamarine
Haemorrhages	Ruby

Haemorroids	Pearl, Coral
Hay Fever	Jet, Zircon
Hair (health of)	Opal, Quartz, Tourmaline, Malachite, Chrysocolla, Smithsonite
Hands (swollen)	Aquamarine, Moonstone
Happiness (promotion of)	Sunstone
Harmony	Opal, Spinel, Rhodonite, Jade, Jadeite, Moonstone
Headache	Turquoise, White Tourmaline, Amber, Jet, Hematite, Emerald
Heart (strengthening of)	Green Garnet, Emerald, Dioptase, Opal, Turquoise
Heartache	Lepidolite, Blue Topaz
Heart attacks (prevention of)	Dolomite, Dioptase
Heartburn	Rock Crystal, Olivine, Dioptase, Emerald
Heart Disease	Ruby, Dioptase
Heart Energy Point (to unblock)	Dioptase, Emerald
Hepatitis	Calcite, Dolomite
Herpes	Dolomite, Jadeite, Lapis Lazuli
Hysteria	Lapis Lazuli, Turquoise
Idealism (promotion of)	Spinel
Idleness	Emerald, Aquamarine, Morganite, Heliodore, Goshenite
Ignorance	Heliodore, Carnelian
Incest (ill effects of)	Lapis Lazuli
Indigestion	Tourmaline, Jasper, Dolomite, Peridot, Bismuth
Indulgence	Bloodstone
Infections	Amethyst, Smoky and Brown Quartz
Inflammations	Topaz, Spinel
Inner growth (encouragement of)	Lapis Lazuli, Chrysoprase
Insanity	Rock Crystal, Citrine, Amethyst, Sard, Topaz
Insomnia	Topaz, Jacinth, Bowenite
Inertia	Zircon
Intellect (improvement of)	Heliodore, Sapphire
Intermittent Fevers	Chrysoprase
Intestine (health of)	Yellow Jasper
Intuition (increase of)	Sapphire, Lapis Lazuli
Invisible Guard	Opal, Sardonyx
Iron Assimilation (into body)	Chrysocolla
Irritability	Rhodonite, Padparadjah

Irritated Throat	Amber, Tourmaline
Irritated Spirit	Spinel
Itching	Malachite, Azurite, Dolomite
Jaundice	Coral, Jadeite
Jealousy	Apophylite
Joint Inflammation	Hematite, Dioptase, Amethyst
Justice (promotion of)	Opal
Kennel Cough (in dogs)	Amber, Jadeite, Hematite, Rock Crystal
Kidney (treatment of)	Nephrite Jade
Laryngitis	Tourmaline, Amber
Legs (to strengthen, make supple)	Aquamarine
Lethargy	Carnelian, Ruby, Tourmaline
Life-force (increase in)	Aquamarine
Lightning (to dispel fear of)	Spinel
Liver (treatment of)	Jasper, Jade, Labradorite, Hiddenite, Emerald, Ruby
Longevity (promotion of)	Diamond
Love (pure, caring, promotion of)	Diamond, Ruby, Pink Sapphire, Rhodonite, Rhodocrosite
Lumbago	Sapphire, Magnetite
Lunacy	River Pebbles, Moonstone, Chalcedony, Rock Crystal, Amethyst, Citrine
Lungs (care of)	Amber
Lung Fluid (to dispel)	Zircon, Diamond, Heliodore, Yellow Sapphire, Amber
Malaria	Turquoise
Malleability of Mind (promotion of)	Aventurine
Malignancy	Alexandrite, Malachite, Azurite, Amethyst, Magnetite, Carnelian, Garnet
Mania	Pearl, Coral, Scapolite
Measles	Pearl, Topaz
Melancholy	Tourmaline, Lapis Lazuli, Sardonyx
Memory	Moss Agate, Emerald, Tourmaline, Pyrolusite
Menopause	Diamond, Ruby
Menstrual Disorders	Topaz, Staurolite, Jet
Mental Burdens	Amethyst
Metabolism (stimulation of)	Sodalite
Migraine	Jet
Mind Strengthener	Zircon

Morality (promotion of)	Jade, Jadeite
Mouth Ailments	Heliodore, Yellow Sapphire
Mumps	Topaz
Multiple Sclerosis	Tourmaline, Blue John, Rose Quartz, Lapis Lazuli, Jadeite all with Gold
Muscles (toning up)	Dolomite, Fluorite, Tourmaline, Spinel, Peridot, Jadeite
Nails (to strengthen)	Pearl, Opal, Calcite, Rhodocrosite
Neck Tension	Alexandrite, Hematite, Magnetite
Negative Energies (to dispel – e.g. to ward off the Evil Eye)	Turquoise, Lapis Lazuli
Negative Energies (stones to avoid if one is prone to sadness, etc.)	Pearl, Azurite, Obsidian
Negativity (to counteract)	Lapis Lazuli
Nephritis	Nephrite Jade
Nerve Cells (healthy activity of)	Chrysoprase
Nerves (to steady and strengthen)	Dolomite, Jade
Nervousness	Lapis Lazuli, Sapphire, Jadeite
Neuritis	Tourmaline
Nightmares	Jet, Turquoise, Padparadjah, Bowenite, Hematite, Ruby
Nobility (reinforcement of tendencies towards)	Opal, Alexandrite, Diamond
Nose Bleeds	Sapphire, Ruby
Nostrils (blocked)	Ambergris, Jet inhalent
Obesity	Tourmaline, Heliodore, Diamond, Zircon
Oral Contraceptive Balancer	Dolomite
Pain (general)	Lapis Lazuli, Ruby, Tourmaline
Pancreas	Jasper, Bloodstone
Passion (to arouse)	Padparadjah, Verdite
Passion (to cool)	Emerald, Blue Sapphire, Amethyst
Perception (to sharpen)	Bowenite, Carnelian
Perspiratory Problems	Jadeite
Physical Harmony (promotion of)	Agatized Coral
Pick-me-up	Blue John
Pigmentation (improvement of)	Chrysocolla
Plague	Ruby, Pearl
Poison (antidote)	Emerald, Unicorn Horn, Zircon
Popularity (to increase)	Turquoise, Citrine
Pregnancy (for strength during)	Chrysolite, Jasper
Protection	Diamond
Purity (to encourage)	Diamond, Jade
Quarrelling (between couples)	Magnetite

Quinsy	Topaz, Amber, Jet
Red Blood cells (to promote health of)	Bornite, Chalcopyrite
Rejuvenator	Irish Fairy Stone
Renal Disease	Jade
Refining Energy (promotion of)	Lapis Lazuli
Rheumatism	Malachite, Azurite, Chrysocolla
Rickets	Calcite, Coral, Pearl
Righteousness	Jade, Jadeite
Ringworm	Diamond, Calcite, Zircon
Sacral Energy Point	Fire Opal, Red Spinel
Sadness	Ruby, Padparadjah
Saliva (excess of)	Diamond, Zircon
Scalding	Emerald
Scar Tissue	Rose Quartz
Sciatica	Sapphire, Tourmaline
Self Expansion	Opal, Zircon, Diamond
Serenity	Jade, Jadeite
Sexual appetite (to arouse and increase)	Padparadjah, Red Amber
Sexual Higher Guidance	Padparadjah
Sexual Impotency and Infertility	Verdite, Padparadjah
Shingles	Jadeite, Lapis Lazuli, Chrysoprase
Sighing	Aquamarine, Emerald, Morganite Goshenite, Heliodore
Sinus	Jet
Skin Colour (to improve)	Hematite
Skin Problems	Sulphur, Topaz, Carbuncle, Pearl, Zircon
Sleeping sickness	Amethyst
Sluggishness	Carnelian, Amethyst
Smell (loss of)	Tourmaline
Snakebite	Emerald, Jasper
Sneezing	Zircon
Solar Plexus Energy Point	Citrine, Heliodore
Solar plexus (cure of ills in)	Sard, Amethyst, Opal, Citrine
Sores	Aventurine, Amethyst, Quartz
Spasms	Carnelian, Dolomite
Spinal Energy Point (to unblock)	Fire Opal, Red Spinel
Spine (general health of)	Jasper, Labradorite, Magnetite, Orange Garnet
Spine (alignment of, i.e. polarization)	Hiddenite, Magnetite, Labradorite
Spleen Energy Point (to unblock)	Orange Zircon, Hessonite, Padparadjah

Stabilizer (promotion of, in mental health)	Onyx, Lapis Lazuli, Azurite
Sterility (to cure)	Red Coral, Padparadjah
Stomach Pains	Lapis Lazuli
Stomach Upsets	Bloodstone, Aquamarine, Emerald, Heliodore, Morganite
Stomach Strengthener	Jasper
Stomach (swollen)	Pearl, Emerald
Strength (to increase)	Magnetite, Ruby
Stress	Dolomite, Spinel
Sunstroke	Chrysoprase, Jadeite
Sweats	Green Sapphire
Taste (improvement of)	Topaz, Tourmaline
Teeth (loose)	Jet
Teeth (strengthening)	Angel Skin and White Coral, Calcite
Telepathy (to induce)	Dioptase, Garnet, Ruby
Tempest (charm against)	Emerald
Tenderness	Rhodonite, Pink Sapphire, Alexandrite, Rose Quartz, Ruby, Kunzite
Third Eye (to open)	Opal, Azurite, Lapis Lazuli, Iolite
Throat (to cure ills in)	Tourmaline, Turquoise, Hematite, Amber
Throat Energy Point (to unblock)	Chrysoprase, Turquoise, Opal
Thyroid (regulation of)	Lapis Lazuli, Rhodonite
Tiredness	Pyrite, Amber
Tonsillitis	Tourmaline, Amber
Toothache	Jet, Amber
Tranquillity (to promote)	Emerald, Jade, Jadeite
Tumours	Jet, Amethyst, Sapphire
Ulcers (eyes)	Sapphire
Ulcers (general)	Tourmaline
Ulcers (skin)	Emerald
Ulcers (stomach)	Sapphire
Unity (promotion of)	Opal
Urinary Ailments	Amber, Jade
Varicose Veins	Aquamarine, Amber, Opal
Venereal Disease	Zircon
Vertigo	Sapphire
Violence	Bloodstone, Rose Quartz
Virtue (to increase)	Jade, Sapphire, Pearl
Vocal Cords (protection of)	Amber, Jet, Tourmaline
Vomiting	Emerald, Lapis Lazuli

Warts	Emerald, or rub with Appatite soaked in Sea Salt
Wasting Disease	Magnetite, Jasper
Weak Muscles	Tourmaline, Moonstone
Weakness (general)	Hematite
Whooping Cough	Amber, Topaz, Coral
Wickedness (evil spells)	Sapphire, Ruby, Opal, Diamond
Wild Beasts (taming of)	Diamond
Will Power (to strengthen)	Ruby, Red Coral, Garnet
Wisdom (promotion of)	Carnelian, Amethyst
Worms	Cassiterite, Ruby
Wounds	Garnet, Ruby

Anniversaries

Anniversaries are important – ask any husband who has forgotten his wife's birthday – and nations as well as individuals celebrate them. So it is not surprising that over the centuries traditions have accumulated linking them with the planets and with particular precious stones.

Here then is another way of associating our lives with the rhythms of the whole universe. Earlier sections of this book have described the stones we should each possess or wear according to our birth signs, as well as those that can help us in sickness and in health because they too harness the planetary powers of which we stand most in need. Owning or carrying the right jewel on the occasion, let us say, of our tenth wedding anniversary or our twenty-fifth or fifty-fifth birthday is no more than an additional way of reinforcing such beneficent influences. It can be fun, too, throwing a party where such stones are worn or displayed. They have the good effect of reminding us of the powers that influence us from outside this Earth, however light-hearted the occasion of that reminder.

The chart printed here shows these connections at a glance – anniversary number, ruling planet, matching stone. But how are they arrived at? If we want to discover this we should look back first of all to the 'Note on Numerology' printed on pages 8 and 9. This states in simple form the law of numerology, according to which all numbers are reduced to single digits, and lists the number traditionally allocated to each planet in our solar system by astrological lore. (The Sun, 1; Mercury, 5; Pluto, 22; and so on.) Once grasped, these two pieces of information make it easy to calculate which planet and which anniversary correspond. For example, a twenty-fifth wedding anniversary will be under the sign of Neptune, because the number astrologically associated with Neptune is 7, and the number of the anniversary, 25, breaks down numerologically in the following way: $2 + 5 = 7$. Now, look back to see what birth sign is ruled by Neptune.

Answer: Pisces. So the stone attributed to the anniversary in question should logically feature among those worn by Pisceans. And so it proves.

Not that everything is completely cut and dried. Why, for instance, Stichtite is designated for an eighth anniversary, corresponding to Saturn's number, and Amethyst for a seventeenth, which is equally Saturn-linked, and not the other way round, is indeed a matter of traditional gemmological wisdom rather than cold logic. But the main principle holds.

One interloper into the column of planets or satellites is Sirius, the Dog-Star, well-known to the sages of Sumeria and Ur of the Chaldees, and to certain primitive African tribes, as already explained. Here it is designated for a fiftieth or hundredth anniversary. For the former, it is fittingly matched with Dioptase, the 'Congo Emerald', both on account of its colour (reflecting those flashes of green emanating from Sirius) and also because the first fine quality crystals of this stone are thought to have been formed at about the time that Sirius was moving closer to Earth. For the latter, it is matched with a red or white Diamond, appropriate to Sirius's colour change, already described, and with a brightness reflecting the Sun ($100 = 1$, the Sun's astrological number). It should also be noted that Lapis Lazuli, a second stone for a centenary, was worn by the priest-seers of Ur and ancient Egypt for the purpose of making contact with Sirius.

For any anniversary over a hundred, tradition dictates a 'Jew's Eye', which, being interpreted, means simply 'any worthy stone'. Well what was good enough for Methuselah....

These additions apart, the chart is self-explanatory, except for the last column which presents a sea of muddles. For the 'Traditional Emblems' for different anniversaries which have reached us down the ages are both illogical and incomplete. Why is there an emblem for a twenty-third anniversary and not for a twenty-fourth? More importantly, what sense are we to make of the value of some of the 'gifts'? Why is china earmarked for a twentieth anniversary when Zircon, Garnet, Amethyst, Topaz, Crystal, Moonstone and even Agate, all more valuable except in rare cases, are specified for the preceding years? What lies behind the choice of modestly priced Coral to mark a thirty-fifth anniversary when a precious Sapphire is to be given for a twenty-third?

These lists have evidently become confused with time, or at least the reasons underlying their arrangement now elude us. And to make confusion worse confounded, several writers on the subject seem to have invented lists of their own. But what matter? Let us practise on the level of national festivities and see how the sums work out.

Are you a patriotic Frenchman of strong republican principles wishing to celebrate the storming of the Bastille on 14th July, 1789 – the famous Quatorze Juillet? If you are throwing your party in the year of grace 1988, you are separated from that historic event by 199 years. So: $1+9+9=19$, and $1+9=10$. You thus know your planet, which is the Sun (astrological number 1); and because the number of intervening years has run right off the chart, you revert to the figure 1 for your anniversary year too. Conclusion: your friends must bring you Sulphur, preferably paper-wrapped.

Perhaps you are English, keen to celebrate the exploits of the only man who went into Parliament with the right idea – Guy Fawkes – and are reading this book in the year 1990. The Gunpowder Plot was discovered on 5th November 1605. Thus the time-lag here will be 385 years and the sum will go as follows: $3+8+5=16$; then $1+6=7$. Conclusion: the ruling planet is Neptune (astrological number 7); and your guests must arrive bearing Apophylite or Native Copper.

Whether you are an American and it is George Washington's Birthday, a Swiss whose National Day commemorates the famous occasion on which William Tell shot the apple from his son's head, or an Australian opening a can of Foster's lager to toast the raising by Captain Cook of the English flag on the shores of Botany Bay, the procedure is the same: follow the rules of numerological calculation, and the chart will do the rest.

One final point. All anniversaries have their significance of course, but the most important day in any of our lives has got to be the one on which we were born. So, while each year may bring its appropriate gift, make sure every baby you know starts off with a present of his or her precious crystal, talisman, and bedside rock.

ANNIVERSARY STONES

ANNIVERSARY PLANET or SATELLITE	MINERALS/ GEMSTONES	TRADITIONAL EMBLEM
1 Sun	Sulphur (wrapped in paper)	Paper (UK, Australia, USA)
2 Moon	Desert Rose	Cotton
3 Jupiter	Chalcopyrite or Bornite	Leather
4 Uranus	Wulfenite * Fossil Leaf	Fruit or Flower (USA)
5 Mercury	Staurolite * Petrified Wood	Wood (UK, USA)
6 Venus	Irish Fairy Stone * Candy Cavern Quartz	Candy (USA), Iron
7 Neptune	Apophylite * Native Copper	Copper (USA) Wool
8 Saturn	Stichtite * Bronzite	Bronze (UK, Australia), Pottery
9 Mars	Jasper * Youngite * Opalized Wood	Willow (USA)
10 Sun	Vanadinite * Cassiterite	Tin (UK, Australia)
11 Moon	Calcite * Pyrite	Steel (USA, Australia)
12 Jupiter	Aurichalcite * Agate	Agate (UK, Australia, USA) Silk, Linen
13 Uranus	Charoite * Moonstone	Moonstone (UK, Australia, USA), Lace
14 Mercury	Vesuvian Lava * Ivory * Moss Agate	Ivory (USA), Moss Agate (UK, Australia)
15 Venus	Marcasite * Rock Crystal	Crystal (UK, Australia, USA)
16 Neptune	Fluorite * Topaz	Topaz (UK, Australia, USA)
17 Saturn	Venus' Hair * Amethyst	Amethyst (UK, Australia, USA)
18 Mars	Bloodstone * Garnet	Garnet (UK, Australia, USA)
19 Sun	Zircon	Zircon (UK, Australia, USA)
20 Moon	Aragonite * Chinastone	China (UK, Australia)

ANNIVERSARY PLANET or SATELLITE	MINERALS/ GEMSTONES	TRADITIONAL EMBLEM
21 Jupiter	Amber	
22 Pluto	Blue John	
23 Mercury	Tektite * Verdite * Sapphire	Sapphire (UK, Australia, USA)
24 Venus	Malachite	
25 Neptune	Satinspar * Native Silver	Silver (UK, Australia, USA) (Diamond Jubilee)
26 Saturn	Jet	
27 Mars	Ruby Zoisite * Bronzite	Bronze (UK, Australia, USA)
28 Sun	Phenacite	
29 Moon	Coral	
30 Jupiter	Chrysocolla * Ivory * Pearl	Ivory (UK), Pearl (Australia, USA)
31 Uranus	Onyx	
32 Mercury	Tiger Eye	
33 Venus	Dioptase	
34 Neptune	Opal Fossil-shape	
35 Saturn	Chonderite * Coral	Coral (UK, Australia, USA)
36 Mars	Bowenite	
37 Sun	Yellow Zircon	
38 Moon	Pearl	
39 Jupiter	Hauyne	
40 Uranus	B.C. Jade * Ruby	Ruby (UK, Australia, USA)
41 Mercury	Uvarovite	
42 Venus	Gem Quality Azurite	
43 Neptune	Chrysoprase	
44 Pluto	Benitoite	
45 Mars	Sunstone * Pink Sapphire	Sapphire (UK, USA, Australia)
46 Sun	White Zircon	
47 Moon	Water Nodule or Selenite	
48 Jupiter	Turquoise	
49 Uranus	Gem quality Cassiterite	
50 Mercury/ Sirius	Labradorite * Dioptase * Native Gold	Gold (UK, Australia, USA) also known as 'Silver Jubilee'

ANNIVERSARY PLANET or SATELLITE	MINERALS/ GEMSTONES	TRADITIONAL EMBLEM
51 Venus	Andalusite	
52 Neptune	Gem Quality Euclase	
53 Saturn	Yellow Topaz	
54 Mars	Morganite	
55 Sun	Heliodor	Emerald
56 Moon	Pearl	
57 Jupiter	Phosphophylite	
58 Uranus	Violane	
59 Mercury	Topazolite	
60 Venus	Star Sapphire * Diamond	Diamond (UK, Australia, USA)
61 Neptune	Hiddenite	
62 Saturn	Lazulite	
63 Mars	Chrysoberyl	
63 Sun	Tsavorite	
65 Moon	Star Rose Quartz	
66 Pluto	Gem Quality Rhodocrosite	
67 Uranus	Gem Quality Tugtupite	
68 Mercury	Iolite	
69 Venus	Green or Lavender Jadeite	
70 Neptune	Blue Diamond	
71 Saturn	Lapis Lazuli	
72 Mars	Gem Quality Rhodonite	
73 Sun	Red Zircon	
74 Moon	Gem Quality Scapolite	
75 Jupiter	Achorite * Yellow Diamond	Diamond (UK, Australia)
76 Uranus	Brazilantine	
77 Mercury	Padparadjah	
78 Venus	Any Colour Spinel	
79 Neptune	Kunzite	
80 Saturn	Tanzanite	
81 Mars	Pink Diamond	
82 Sun	Gem Quality Spene	
83 Moon	Adularia	
84 Jupiter	Bi-Colour Tourmaline	

ANNIVERSARY PLANET or SATELLITE	MINERALS/ GEMSTONES	TRADITIONAL EMBLEM
85 Uranus	Diopside	
86 Mercury	Cat's Eye	
87 Venus	Kashmir Sapphire	
88 Pluto	Pigeon's Blood Ruby and Erythrite	
89 Saturn	Opal Pineapple	
90 Mars	Pink Sapphire	
91 Sun	Blue (Heat treated) Zircon	
92 Moon	Water Opal	
93 Jupiter	Melonstone	
94 Uranus	Olive Green Peridot	
95 Mercury	Black Opal	
96 Venus	Emerald	
97 Neptune	Aquamarine	
98 Saturn	Pink Topaz	
99 Mars	Alexandrite	
100 Sun/Sirius	Red or White Diamond, Lapis Lazuli	

* Denotes traditional stone or token.

Envoi

Around the early years of this century there flourished among the Sioux Indians a famous Medicine Man called Tantanka-Ohitika. In his youth he had received a vision which he loved to describe and which he recorded like this.

'At the age of ten I looked at the land and rivers, the animals and the sky above, and could not fail to realize that some great power had made them. I was so anxious to understand this power that I questioned the trees, the bushes and the flowers. Studying the mossy stones I saw that some seemed to have human features. Afterwards I dreamt that one of these stones appeared and said that by my quest to know the Creator, I had shown myself worthy of supernatural help. When in future, said the stone, I was curing the sick I had only to call upon its assistance and it would command all the forces of nature to aid me.'

This vision, now known as Tantanka-Ohitika's 'Dream of the Sacred Stone', is the note on which the author of this book wishes to take leave of her readers. Stones and gems are one of Nature's precious gifts. They bring healing and harmony, wisdom and courage, cheerfulness, generosity and joy, and their beauty enriches the world. They are given for our pleasure. Let us use and understand them to the full.

Acknowledgements

First, thanks must go to Christopher Baker who devoted much of his time to the conception and the whole manuscript, and who provided the peaceful environment needed during my years of research and writing. I wish the completion of this book to be partly his pride. Equal gratitude must go to Rivers Scott, who managed to unravel my mêlée of tangled sentences and skilfully wove them into an understandable whole. His ingenuity is only overshadowed by his Etonian charm and my debt.

Special acknowledgement is due to Gary Lundquist for helping me with my calculations on the constituent elements of planets, and for his comprehensive range of knowledge. Few scientists would have bothered as he did with the layman's point of view. I also deeply appreciate the help given to me by Roger Harding, Curator of Gems at the British Museum, who nurtured my interest in the myriad, exquisite crystals not usually brought to public attention. His careful explanations and patience never flagged.

Geologists Lin and Martin Searle dug deep for the infinitesimal detail I often required. Their long discussions went beyond the call of friendship. I am grateful for the information supplied by Fred Birnie on his speciality of Jade and Jadeite, and by Helen Fraquer on amber and other minerals; also to Denis Inkersole of the City of London Polytechnic for his expertise in class and to Rex Dallimore and Helen Muller who gave me the benefit of their knowledge of Opals and Jet respectively.

Pamela Towlson generously extended her hospitality at the Royal Astronomical Society, allowing me to spend many hours sifting through records, books and photographs in its wonderful library and letting me pick her brains. Most of all I thank her for remembering my cause and keeping me posted with snippets of interest.

I received much helpful advice on the Western school of astrology from Betina Lee and Jeff Meddle, who were attached to the London Astrological Lodge; and, on the Indian school from Manika Ghosh. My thanks too to John Clarke of the Sydney Astrological Centre. To all three time had no importance.

John Pyeman opened the floodgates of knowledge about the science of self-discipline and offered me valuable facts on mythology, numerology and other key matters. Georgia Pitsillides contributed information on soluble minerals, vitamins and amino acids which helped me enormously in the section on healing.

My grateful acknowledgements also go to the many patients and healers I consulted, particularly Vera Van Der Sleesen, Elizabeth Draper, Gordon Prangley and Dunstan Harrison – the last two as workers concerned with the remarkable gem lamp at Bath, England. Thanks to them, I benefited personally from this, and was then allowed to observe the treatment of individual patients, including an active little boy once condemned by orthodox medics to a short, confined lifestyle he had long outlived.

Heartfelt thanks for help and encouragement of various kinds go to Diana Howard Campi, Sylvia Compton Miller, Marie Laure Lawson, Margaret Breton, Pauline Baker, Patrick Crosbie, Michael Sinel, Diana Howard Campi's doctor, and an unknown professor at the Greek University; to Christine Motley for her valiant typing; to my mother, Margaret Goodall, and to Gabriela Ebert, Sheila McErlane, and Barbara Sarik.

Likewise to Oliver Caldecott, who believed in the value of the subject and brought out the stubborn streak which enabled me to finish this task; and to Gloria Ferris who made light of dark days and who, through truth, gentle probing and an occasional crack of the whip brought my brain into focus.

Finally this work would never have grown beyond its embryo stage without the enthusiastic support, advice and loving care given to me by Veronica Dickinson.

Bibliography

Atkinson, Richard and Frances, *The Observer's Book of Rocks and Minerals* (William Clowes & Sons Ltd, Beccles & London).

Bariand, Paul (texts) and Bariand, Nelly (photographs) *The Wonderful World of Precious Stones in Their Natural State* (Abbey Library, London).

Bible, Old and New Testaments, Standard and Revised edns.

Browning, Robert, *The Byzantine Empire* (Weidenfeld & Nicolson, London).

Bruton, Eric, Diamonds (2nd edn. NAD Press Ltd, London).

Burland, C. A. *Peoples of the Sun* (Weidenfeld & Nicolson, London).

Child, John, *Australian Rocks and Minerals* (Periwinkle Press, 1963; rev. and enlarged edn, Landsdowne Press, Melbourne, 1969).

Crow, W. B. *Precious Stones* (Aquarian Press).

David, Dr Rosalie (ed.), *Mysteries of the Mummies* (The story of the Manchester University investigation) (Book Club Associates).

Dixon, Don, *Universe* (Houghton Mifflin, Boston).

Gubelin, Eduard, *Precious Stones* (3rd edn, Hallwag, Berne, 1973).

Kirkaldy, J. F. *Minerals and Rocks* (Blandford Press, London).

Leland, Charles Godfrey, *Gypsy Sorcery and Fortune Telling* (Dover Publications, New York).

Lons, Veronica, *The World's Mythology in Colour* (Hamlyn, London).

McLintock, W. F. P., *Gemstones in the Geological Museum*, 4th edn rev. Patricia M. Statham, based on 3rd edn, rev. P. A. Sabine (1951, 4th 1983).

Mailard, Robert (ed.), *Diamonds, Myth, Magic and Reality* (Crown Publishers, New York).

Malin, David and Murdin, Paul, *Colours of the Stars* (Cambridge University Press, Cambridge).

Mineralogical Record, The, *Tourmaline – 1* (Mineralogical Record Inc.).

Murray, Margaret A., *The Splendour that was Egypt* (Sidgwick & Jackson, London).

Ollerenshaw, Arthur E., *Blue John Cavern and Blue John Mine* (no further details available).

Ollerenshaw, Arthur E., *The History of Blue John Stone* (no further details available).

Poynder, Michael, *The Price Guide to Jewellery 3000 BC– 1950 AD* (Antique Collector's Club Ltd, Suffolk).

Read, H. H., *Rutley's Elements of Mineralogy* (Thomas Murby, London).

Royal Astronomical Society, numerous reference books.

Sauer, Jules Roger, *Brazil: Paradise of Gemstones* (Jules Roger Sauer, 1982).

Silverman, David P., *The Masterpieces of Tutankhamun*, Introduction and commentaries (Abbeville Press, New York).

Temple, Robert K. G., *The Sirius Mystery* (Billing & Sons, Guildford and London).

Woolley, Dr Alan (ed.), *Mineral Kingdom* (Hamlyn, London).

Wright, Esmond (ed.), *The Ancient World* (Hamlyn, London, 1969, rev. and updated 1979; Chartwell Book Sales Inc. New Jersey).

List of Suppliers

Below is a list of some of the best crystal, rock and gem sellers in England and Australia

England
Jewellers
Elizabeth Gage
20 Albemarle St
London W1

Crystal, Rock and Gem retailers
R. Holt and Co.
98 Hatton Garden
London EC1

Gregory, Bottley & Lloyd
8–12 Rickett St
London SW6 1RU

Glenjoy
19–21 Sun Lane
Wakefield
West Yorks.

Sam Weller Minerals
Pendeen
West Cornwall

Caverswall Minerals
The Dams
Caverswall
Stoke-on-Trent
Staffs.

Isis Minerals
Ironbridge Works
Marlborough Rd
Accrington
Lancs.

Malvern Lapidary
39 Broadlands Drive
Malvern
Worcs. WR14 1PW

Australia
Jewellers
Ladybird Gem Merchants
Shop 77
1st gallery level
The Strand Arcade
Sydney
NSW 2000

Cyril Kovac
Gemcraft Proprietary Ltd.
1st Floor
293 Wattle Tree Road
East Malvern
Victoria 3145

Clark the Jeweller
115a Rundle Mall
Adelaide
S Australia 5000

Bruce Mazzuccelli
City Arcade
Perth
W Australia 6000

*Crystal, Rock and Gem
retailers*
The Rock Shop
M. I. and C. J. Parkinson
Arcade 83
Shop 4
83 Longueville Rd
Lane Cove
Sydney NSW 2066

Peter Hunt
Crystals Australia (Aboriginal
Mined)
PO Box 53
Northcote
Victoria 3070
S Australia

Lapidary Suppliers
100A Henley Beach Road
Mile End
S Australia

Opal Time
Rex Dallimore
3191 Gold Coast Highway
Surfer's Paradise
Queensland 4217

The Rock Shop
Currumbin Bird Sanctuary
Currumbin
Gold Coast
Queensland

Rene Boisseivain
69 Main St
Atherton Tableland
Queensland

The Rockhole
Rieff's Building
50 Hartley St
Alice Springs
Northern Territory 5750

The Gem Cave
85 Todd Street
Alice Springs 5750
Western Australia

Perth Lapidary and Gift
Centre
58 Pier St
Perth
Western Australia 6000

Westway Gems
Christine Boeswirth
730 Rosedale Rd
Chidlow
Western Australia

Index

Page numbers in *italic* refer to the illustrations

absent healing, 108
Adamite, 65, 111
Adularia, 44
Agate, *23*, 49, 159
  Banded, 3
  Blue Lace, *23*, 96
  Moss, 40–1
  see also Sardonyx
Agatized Coral, 126
Alamandine Garnet, 56
Albert, Prince Consort, 83, 96
Alexander II, Tsar, 28
Alexander the Great, 96, 136
Alexandra, Queen, 51
Alexandrite, 27–8, 68, 117
Amber, 5, *23*, 75 6, 83, 112, 117–18
Amethyst, 3, 7, *22*, *23*, 43, 59, 70,
  85, 108, 111, 118, 119, 123, 125–
  6, 159
  Oriental, 70
Ammonite, Pyritized, 36
Andalusite, 33–4
anniversaries, 158–64
Apophylite, 98, 111, 160
Aquamarine, 52, 81, 93, 107, 111,
  116, 119–20, 122, 136
Aquarius, 18, 20, 87–93
Aragonite, 48
Ariel, 19
Aries, 6, 16, 27–32
Arizona, 56
auras, 107
Aurichalcite, 78, 111
Ava, King of, 74
Aventurine, 89, 120–1
Azurite, *23*, 35, 111, 116, 121

Banded Agate, 3
Bedouin, 49
bedside rocks, 6
  Aquarius, 91–3
  Aries, 31–2
  Cancer, 48–9
  Capricorn, 85–6
  Gemini, 42–4
  Leo, 53–4

Libra, 64–6
Pisces, 96–8
Sagittarius, 78–9
Scorpio, 71–2
Taurus, 36–8
Virgo, 59–60
Belamnites, 97
Benitoite, 67–8
Beryl, 28
Bible, 4, 66
Black Opal, 55
Bloodstone, 119, 121–2
  see also Heliotrope; Hematite
Blue Diamond, 127
Blue Earth, 50
Blue John, 69, 122
Blue Lace Agate, *23*, 96
Bonamite, 95
Bone Turquoise, 78
Bornite, 79, 111, 123–4
Bottlestone, 60
Bouron, Count de, 74
Bowenite, 29–30, 123
Brazilian Rocket, 74
Brazilianite, 87
Brown Quartz, 85

Calcite, *22*, *23*, 48, 111
calendar, 5–6
Cancer, 13, 44–9
Capricorn, 18, 80–6
Carbuncle, 56
Carnelian, 30, 84, 119, 120, 123,
  134, 135
Casiterite, 91
Catherine of Aragon, 66
Catherine the Great, 75
Cat's Eye, 39–40
Cat's Eye Scapolite, 44–5
Ceyloite, 61
chakras, 108, *110*
Chalcopyrite, *22*, 79, 111, 123–4
Charoite, 92
Charon, 21–4
Chiastolite, 34
Chondrolite, 81
Chrysoberyl, 40
Chrysocolla, 78–9, 111, 124
Chrysolite, 87

Chrysoprase, 96, 123, 125
Cinnabar, 31
Citrine, *23*, 81, 85, 111, 125–6
cleaning stones, 109–14
Cleopatra, 32
colour, energy through, 108–9
Confucius, 39
Congo Emerald *see* Dioptase
Copper, 160
Copper Emerald *see* Dioptase
Coral, 5, 47, 48, 112, 126, 159
    Agatized, 126
Cornelian *see* Carnelian
corundrum, 38–9
Crawford Centre, 104
Crocoite, 71
Crystal, 159
    see also Rock Crystal

Deimos, 15
Desert Rose, 48–9, 111
Diamond, 7, 20, 53, 93, 98, 112–13,
    126–7, 141–2, 143, 146, 147, 159
    Blue, 127
    hardness, 8, 9
    Kerry, 85
    Pink, 27
    White, 50–1, 81
    Yellow, 49–50, 127
Diopside, 88–9
Dioptase, 63, 107, 112, 122, 128,
    135, 143, 159
Dogtooth Calcite, 48
Dolomieu, Deodat, 31
Dolomite, 31, 138

Earth, 13, 15, 24
Edward, Black Prince, 61
Edward the Confessor, 119
Eilat (Elath) Stone, *22*, 76, 124
Electron *see* Amber
Elizabeth, Queen Mother, 51
Elizabeth I, Queen, 46, 136
Elizabeth II, Queen, 69
Emerald, 28, 32–3, 52, 113, 128,
    129, 143
    Copper *see* Dioptase
    Oriental, 33
    Red, 33

energy through colour, 108–9
Enhydrous, 49
esoteric cleansing, 113–14
Euclase, 94–5
Evening Emerald *see* Peridot

Fabergé, Carl, 28, 30, 89, 120
Fir Cones, Opalized, 97
Flèche d'Amour, 86
Fletcher, Aaron, 104
Flos Ferri, 48
Fluorite, 97–8, 111, 112, 115
Fool's Gold, 37
Fossil Wood, 97
Fossils, Opalized, 96–7
Frederick II, Emperor, 51
Friedman Study, 104

Garnet, 87, 130, 143, 144, 159
    Alamandine, 56
    Pyrope, 50
    Spessartine, 57
    Transvaal Jade, 41–2
    Uvarovite, 41
Gemini, 6, 14, 38–44
gemstones, 6–7
Geode, *22*, *23*, 43–4
George III, King, 20
Green Earth, 29, 40, 43
Grey, Lady Jane, 46
Gypsum, *22*

Halite, 111
Hallowes, Odette, 114
Hauyne, 78
Hawkins, Mr, 67
Hawk's Eye, 58
healers, 104, 105
Heliodore, *52*, 130–1
Heliotrope, 29
Hematite, *22*, 29, 112, 135, 141
    Specular, 59
Henry VIII, King, 46
Herschel, Sir John, 19–20
Hidden, A.E., 94
Hiddenite, 94
holistic medicine, 103–4
Homer, 54

Iceland Spar, 48
Ilmenite, 66
Imperial Green Jadeite, 63–4
Inca Rose *see* Rhodocrosite
Io, 17, 53
Iolite, 55–6
Irish Fairy Stone, 37–8
Iron Pyrites, *23*

Jacinth, 51
Jade, *23*, 90–1, 112, 131–2
Jadeite, 35–6, 90, 112, 125, 131–2, 143
    Imperial Green, 63–4
Jargon, 51
Jasper, 29, 31–2, 86, 132
Jet, 5, 82–3, 112, 132–3
John the Divine, St, 86
Jupiter, 4, 6, 8, 9, 11, 16–17, 28

Kashmir Sapphire, 62
Kerry Diamond, 85
Kidney Ore, 59
Kish, King of, 83
Koh-i-Noor, 50–1
Korean Jade *see* Bowenite
Kunz, Dr G.F., 94
Kunzite, 94
Kyanite, 61, 64

Labradorite, 57, 107, 133
Lapis Lazuli, 3, *23*, 83–4, 88, 92, 113, 133–4, 135, 143, 146, 159
Lava, Vesuvian, 58
Lazulite, 83
Leo, 11, 49–54
Lepidocrite, 29
Lepidolite, 43
Libra, 15, 61–6
life-force, 107
Limonite, 65
Lithia Emerald, 94
Lodestone *see* Magnetite

Magnetite, 59–60, 122, 134–5
Malachite, *22*, *23*, 35, 111, 121, 135
Malacom, 51
Marcasite Dollar, 36–7
Mark Antony, 70

Mars, 3, 6, 8, 9, 10, 11, 15–16, 24, 27
Mary, Queen, 51
Matura, 51
meditation, 114–16
Melonstone, 73
Mercury (metal), 31
Mercury (planet), 3, 6, 8, 9, 10, 11, 13–14
Meterorite, 60
Mica, *23*, 50
Milky Way, 4, 10, 11
Miranda, 19
Mocha Stones, 40–1
Mohs, Friedrich, 8
Mohs scale of hardness, 8–9
Moon, 4, 8, 10, 12–13, 24
Moonstone, 7, *23*, 44, 135, 159
Morion, 85
Moses, 116
Moss Agate, 40–1
Mother-of-Pearl, 46, 112
Mountain Mahogany, 60
Mtorodite, 125
Mugford, Roger, 104
Mullite, 64
Muscovite, 53

Nailhead Calcite, 48
NASA, 11
Natrolite, 111
Neptune, 8, 9, 10, 11, 17, 20–1, 24
Nero, Emperor, 69
New Mexico Ruby, 56
Nicholas, Tsarevitch, 30
Nicholas II, Tsar, 141
numerology, 8–9, 158–9

Oberon, 19
Obsidian, 60, 135–6
Okenite, 72
Olivine, 50
Onomacritus, 45
Onyx, 89
Opal, 7, *23*, 43, 78, 79, 111–12, 114, 136–7
    Black, 55
    Water, 45–6
    White, 55

Opal Pineapple, 81–2
Opalized Fossil, 96–7
Orange Sapphire, 38–9, 142
Oriental Amethyst, 70
Oriental Emerald, 33

Padparadjah, 38–9, 142
Peacock Ore, 79
Pearl, 4, 5, 46, 112, 138
Pearl Spar *see* Dolomite
Peridot, 9, 87, 139, 143
pets, 104
Phenacite, 51–2
Phobos, 15
Phosphophylite, 74
Pigeon's Blood, 66–7
Pink Sapphire, 9
Pisces, 17, 21, 93–9
Plasma, 29
Pliny the Elder, 45, 69
Pluto, 8, 10, 11, 16, 21–4
Polo, Marco, 84
Potato Stone *see* Geode
'power-house' position, meditation, 115
precious crystals, 6
    Aquarius, 87–9
    Aries, 27–8
    Cancer, 44–9
    Capricorn, 80–2
    Gemini, 38–40
    Leo, 49–51
    Libra, 61–3
    Pisces, 93–5
    Sagittarius, 73–5
    Scorpio, 66–8
    Taurus, 32–4
    Virgo, 55–7
Prehnite, 72
Pu-Abi, Queen, 83–4
Pyrite, 37
Pyritized Ammonite, 36
Pyrope Garnet, 50

Quartz, 7, *23*, 31, 72, 85, 86
    Brown, 85
    Rose, 46–7, 121, 136, 141
    Rutilated, 86
    Smoky, *23*, 85

Star Rose, 47
Quetzalcoatl, 14

Rasputin, 141
Reagan, Ronald, 91
Rhodocrosite, *22*, 68, 107, 139
Rhodonite, 28, 107, 139–40
Rock Crystal, 3, 7, *22*, 43, 51–2, 72, 78, 79, 81, 86, 106, 107, 111, 114, 116, 121, 140–1, 143
Rose Quartz, *22*, 46–7, 121, 136, 141
Rose Topaz, 81
Rubellite, 43
Ruby, 7, 61, 66–7, 88, 113, 141–2, 143
    Star, 67
Ruby Zoisite, 32
Rudolph II, Kaiser, 75
Ruskin, John, 73
Rutilated Quartz, 86

Sagittarius, 17, 73–9
Sanders, T. Edwin, 67
Sapphire, 7, 33, 61–2, 68, 113, 142, 143, 159
    Kashmir, 62
    Orange, 38–9, 142
    Oriental Amethyst, 70
    Pink, 26
    Star, 62, 142
    White, 81
Sard *see* Carnelian
Sardonyx, *23*
Star Ruby, 67
Star Sapphire, 62, 142
Starstone, 62
Staurolite, 42
Stibnite, 71
Stichtite, 85, 159
Sulphur, *23*, 54, 111, 160
Sumerians, 3–4
Sun, 4, 6, 8, 9, 10–11
Sunstone, 29, 120

Taafeite, 39
talismans, 6
    Aquarius, 89–91
    Aries, 29–30

Cancer, 46–7
Capricorn, 82–4
Gemini, 40–2
Leo, 51–2
Libra, 63–4
Pisces, 95–6
Sagittarius, 75–6
Scorpio, 69–70
Taurus, 35–6
Virgo, 57–8
Tantanka-Ohitika, 165
Tanzanite, 81
Taurus, 15, 32–8
Tennyson, Alfred, Lord, 82
Thatcher, Margaret, 91
Thunder Egg, 79
Tiffany & Co., 63
Tiger's Eye, 23, 58
Timor Ruby, 61
Titania, 19
Topaz, 80–1, 107, 113, 144, 159
  Rose, 81
  White, 61
Torbenite, 92–3
Tourmaline, 7, 73–5, 111, 144–5
Transvaal Jade, 41–2
Triton, 21
Tsavorite, 63
Tugtupite, 88–9
Turquoise, 7, 23, 76–8, 112, 145–6
Tutankhamun, 60
Tz'e Hsi, Empress Dowager, 36

Umbriel, 19
Uranus, 6, 8, 10, 11, 18, 19–20
Uvarovite Garnet, 41

Vanadinite, 53
Venus, 3, 6, 8, 10, 11, 13, 14–15
Venus' Hair, 86
Verdite, 42–3
Vesuvian Lava, 58
vibrations, 108
Victoria, Queen, 50, 83, 136
Violane, 88
Violet Diopside, 88
Virgo, 14, 55–60
Volcanic Bombs, 54

Water Nodule, 49
Water Opal, 45–6
Water Sapphire see Iolite
Wavellite, 65
Wen Di, Emperor, 90
White Diamond, 50–1, 81
White Opal, 55
White Sapphire, 81
White Topaz, 61
Wong, Davis, 91
Wood, Fossil, 97
Wulfen, Father F., 92
Wulfenite, 91–2

Yellow Citrine, 81
Yellow Diamond, 49–50, 127
Youngite, 31–2

'Zebra', 58
Zibirat see Peridot
Zircon, 7, 51, 107, 113, 143, 146–7,
  159

About the Author

Magda Palmer was born in Melbourne, Australia. She has worked as a commercial artist, television presenter and newsreader. Her abiding passion, however, has been gemstones. She has been researching the subject in depth over the past nine years and this book is the result. For some years she worked as a consultant on the mythological associations and healing properties of gems for 'Nature Sculpture' a shop-within-a-shop at Harrods. She also gave customers an idea of stones which are appropriate in respect of their birth signs and anniversaries, useful in healing and to keep by their bedside. At present, Magda Palmer lives in Australia, where she has appeared frequently on TV in commercials and other programmes.